# Life After Debt

Peter Phillips

# Life After Debt

### Peter Phillips

*All the profits from this publication are being donated to Prostate UK and Pancreas Research at Liverpool, registered charities.*

Matador
5 Weir Road
Kibworth Beauchamp
Leicester LE8 0LQ, UK
Tel: (+44) 116 279 2299
Fax: (+44) 116 279 2277
Email: books@troubador.co.uk
Web: www.troubador.co.uk/matador

ISBN 978 1848765 269

British Library Cataloguing in Publication Data.
A catalogue record for this book is available from the British Library.

Front cover cartoon © Ken Pyne - Nisyndication.com / 21st March 1991.

The originals of all the cartoons in this book were purchased by Peter
Phillips and where possible he has contacted the original artists who
have given their permission.

The source of all press cuttings is acknowledged.

Some of the quotes are not attributed to anybody. This is because
after extensive research, the origin could not be located.

Matador is an imprint of Troubador Publishing Ltd
Printed in the UK by TJ International Ltd, Padstow, Cornwall

## Acknowledgements and Dedications

There would have been no stories to write without Bernard and Percy Phillips.

There would have been no book without the encouragement and love of Wendy, Leo and Kira, the energy and faith of James Miller and the fast fingers of Fenella Berman.

# Contents

Life After Debt

'*Capitalism without bankruptcy would be like Christianity without Hell*'

William Bourke, Executive Vice-President, Ford Motor Company

## A Personal Foreword By Peter Joyce CB

Almost from the first day in October 1960 that I walked along a bustling Carey Street, passed by the Royal Courts of Justice and stepped into the musty, gloomily lit, stone-floored corridors of Bankruptcy Buildings to join the Government Insolvency Service (Official Receivers), I had heard many working in insolvency talking of writing a book about the cases they had dealt with and the stories to be told of bankrupts and directors involved in them. Indeed, it has been suggested to me on more than one occasion that I might undertake such an enterprise covering my time in the rather unusual world of insolvency (although more recently become rather too usual, and painfully so, for too many people).

But I had not the wit and wisdom of Peter Phillips to maintain notations and jottings which might have aided a memory of proceedings and people; nor, and perhaps as importantly, the consummate skill in telling stories, shortly, interestingly and amusingly. Some may say that others who had spoken of putting pen to paper may also have lacked one or more of those attributes - I, in that time honoured phrase supposed to be much used by us civil servants, could not possibly comment. Or perhaps it needed just a little touch of magic, for amongst his many talents Peter is a member of the Magic Circle. And so, this is one of the rare collections of such tales to be told - or certainly to appear in print - over my and his fifty years.

My own career in the public sector pretty much ran alongside Peter's as a private sector insolvency practitioner. By a curiosity one of the first insolvency practitioners I met from 'the other side' was his father. Bernard Phillips, tall, immaculately suited, gentlemanly, and with a great knowledge and understanding of the arcana of insolvency, regularly attended at Bankruptcy Buildings to pick up papers relating to cases to which he had been appointed as trustee in place of the official receiver; and frequently treated me (and it was a treat), a young and somewhat callow trainee examiner, to illuminating insights into case law and practice, offered and not pressed and always in a kindly avuncular manner.

Like father like son then (except the avuncular bit when it came to Peter since we were, and still are of course, of an age). Our paths crossed from time to time at both work and social levels, and very much came together in 1988-89 when first, he was elected President of the Insolvency Practitioners Association to lead the insolvency profession; and then, I was appointed Inspector General to head The Insolvency Service.

It should not however be supposed that it has all been plain sailing – always between us but not always for us. By another co-incidence the recession of the first half of the 1990s saw me appearing before, and being excoriated by, the House of Commons Public Accounts Committee (over The Insolvency Service's performance, for want of resources, in relation to the disqualification of directors of failed companies); and he appearing before, and being in his words savaged by, the Social Security Select Committee (over the Maxwell Receivership – see pages xx-xx). We survived our experiences; and Peter being subsequently exonerated (well, to the extent of 99.6%), it was the greatest pleasure to see him being invested with the OBE in the New Year's Honours 2004 for services to the insolvency profession: even *Accountancy Age* seemed to enjoy the award.

# Life After Debt

By then, by a further turn of events, I had retired from The Insolvency Service and taken a part time appointment with the Insolvency Practitioners Association where I had the opportunity to work with Peter, who for many years served on its Council and Committees, and to very readily see why his OBE was entirely and fittingly justified. He has now retired but I continue to 'take wine', along with excellent luncheons, in the company of the eminent Past President.

But, you may ask, what about the book? It is, I think, a jolly good read, offering 'not a lot of people know that' perspectives of the collapse (and in a few cases, resurrection) of many household names, as well as conjuring up (sic) some 'blasts from the past'; and providing Peter's own lighter, personal pictures of what lay behind starker and more severe headlines of financial failure. Without this record, those pictures would be lost, as indeed would many of the cases themselves other than in dry and dusty law reports; as would the infectious, and affectionate, nature of Peter himself. Enjoy!

*Peter Joyce was Inspector General of the Government Insolvency Service 1989-2001; was Chairman and then Executive Director of the Inter-Governmental International Association of Insolvency Regulators 1985-2008; and is Director General of the Insolvency Practitioners Association.*

---

And by yet another of those co-incidences, as I approach my fifty years so the Insolvency Practitioners Association, which Peter and I have served in different capacities, will follow in reaching its fifty years in 2011. Started as a discussion group for those involved in sorting out financial failure, it became the body for insolvency professionals and has led the way in setting standards, establishing and extending access to qualifications, engaging debate on the insolvency issues and modernising regulation. August 2010

# A Little Bit of Background

Life After Debt

# On Track of Tanfield's Gold and Jewels

## "Startling Developments" Expected By Bankruptcy Official

CREDITORS of Stanley William Tanfield, the convicted share-pusher, who is now serving seven years penal servitude in Wormwood Scrubs, may be paid 20s. in the £ if new lines of inquiry, begun to-day, are successful.

The trustees in the bankruptcies of Tanfield and his wife expect "startling developments" during the next four days in their widespread search for the hidden hoard of gold and jewellery which Tanfield accumulated shortly before his arrest.

Claims against Tanfield total £40,000 and against his wife £20,000.

### More Clues

Valuable information was received to-day by the Trustees from more anonymous telephone - callers and anonymous letter-writers, claiming to be former associates of Tanfield.

All day long Mr. Bernard Phillips, one of the trustees, had gone to different addresses in London, following up inquiries.

To-morrow he is flying to Paris to make contact with safe deposit managers and other people who have been making inquiries for him.

Every safe deposit in England and France has been requested to tell the trustees whether or not Tanfield holds a safe deposit.

The trustees have secured a number of possible aliases in which Tanfield have hidden away his hoard, and names are being checked up with people.

Mr. Bernard Phillips.

mise to be most valuable of all the evidence we have been given.

"You may take it that there will be startling developments within the next four days.

"If our plans work out as we expect they will, creditors will be paid twenty shillings in the pound. Mrs. Tanfield's examination in bankruptcy comes before the court on October 18, and she will no doubt attend then.

"I have received a doctor's certificate from Paris, saying that she is at present unwell and may not be fit enough to attend the court on September 1, when her husband's bankruptcy is to be gone into.

*Evening News* – 19th August 1938

-2-

## A Little Bit of Background

My paternal great grandparents fled the Pogroms in Russia at the end of the 19th century. They arrived at Liverpool docks under the name Levkovitch and were advised by an immigration officer that Levkovitch would not go down too easily in the UK.

The officer offered them the surname that we now use. My grandparents' eldest child, Percy, was born in 1900 and the last of their five children, my father Bernard, was born in 1914.

Those two generations lived, like many others of similar origins, in extreme poverty in the East End of London. Percy, the first to go out to work, at sixteen, studied in the evenings until he qualified as a Certified Accountant five years later. This enabled him to fund Dad's apprenticeship (or, as the profession then called it, Articles of Clerkship) at a firm of chartered accountants. He qualified at the age of twenty-one.

Bernard and Percy forthwith began a remarkable professional partnership which lasted over fifty years. (Look at the two dates on the press cuttings pp 2 and 4.) Whilst, during its first years, their firm supplied general accounting services, after the Second World War ended, the level of insolvencies, both personal and corporate, began to demand some specialist practitioners. Just as the late Sir Kenneth Cork and his late brother, Norman, became eminent insolvency practitioners in the City of London, Bernard and Percy were their peers in the West End of London.

After an unimpressive performance at Highgate School and a period of time in Paris, where I learnt little more than the language and how to play the guitar, Dad suggested that it was

The great and the good of the insolvency world were paraded at London's Glaziers' Hall last week for the retirement thrash of one of its leading figures. Bernard Phillips, most recently head of Arthur Andersen's insolvency department, retired after more than 50 years in the business. Phillips, who is pictured here (centre) along with that other major figure among receivers and liquidators, Sir Kenneth Cork (right) and Norman Cork who was for years the senior partner of the family specialist insolvency firm up to its merger with Arthur Andersen in 1982.

Until recently the Phillips clan held a dominant position with Andersen – son Peter left earlier this year as senior partner of the insolvency practice. Father, however, is expected to keep up the connection, continuing at 73 to work one day a week at the firm.

*Accountancy Age* – 18th August 1988

time to take life seriously. In the early 1960s, most of my contemporaries took what their fathers said seriously. I did also by serving my Articles of Clerkship with mine. By the time I qualified as a Chartered Accountant I had already spent a number of years specialising in the insolvency work handled at 76 New Cavendish Street, London, W1. Qualification brought with it an opportunity to take appointments as Liquidator, Receiver or Trustee in Bankruptcy, in the same way as my father and uncle, to whom I truly owe anything I may be thought to have achieved in my forty-two year career.

In 1979, Bernard Phillips & Co, the practice in which the three Phillips worked, began its merger with, the then, most revered and feared accounting practice in the world, Arthur Andersen. This happened at exactly the same time as Sir Kenneth Cork's practice, Cork Gully, merged with Coopers & Lybrand (now PricewaterhouseCoopers).

I was appointed head of Arthur Andersen's first ever insolvency division and their first ever insolvency partner. I left them in 1988 and with David Buchler, who had become my articled clerk at Bernard Phillips & Co in 1970, formed Buchler Phillips and moved back into our beloved West End of London. I was Chairman of Buchler Phillips until it was acquired in 1999 by Kroll, a listed US corporation, which retained my services until my retirement in 2005.

It is interesting to match this chronology with the evolution of the insolvency profession itself. What we now know as the Accounting and Auditing professions came into existence with the first use of 'Accounting Type Persons' at the end of the 19th century to deal with insolvencies. With the emergence of taxation at the beginning of the 20th century and the rapid development of auditing services, very little, if any, interest was then shown in the world of insolvency by the major accounting firms until the early 1970s. By that time the extremely active world of personal bankruptcies and company collapses was being serviced by an increasingly well organised and professional community of smaller practitioners and firms nationwide. There being so little general guidance to practitioners in this field and such jurisprudence as there was being initiated by the practitioners themselves, a Social and Discussion Group specialising in insolvency had formed itself into a quasi association in 1961. Percy was the second chairman of that discussion group and Bernard followed not very many years later. I tagged onto my father's coat tails for my first meeting of the group in 1962 in Belgrave Square in London.

With no encouragement or indeed pressure from outside, that group metamorphosed into the insolvency practitioners Association in the 1970s and introduced an ethical guide and a requirement for entry by examination, in the first significant attempt to regulate the activities of those calling themselves Insolvency Practitioners, a term finally adopted in statute in the 1986 Insolvency Act.

Mega failures like Courtline, Horizon Holidays and, of course, Rolls Royce sucked in the vast manpower resources of the big accounting firms in the 1970s most of which firms jump started their skill base with acquisitions of small specialist practices (like mine) or of individual practitioners.

With the Insolvency Act of 1986 and the licensing of Insolvency Practitioners came the long overdue recognition of Insolvency

Practice as a profession in its own right. At this point in history, an insolvency profession that consists of mostly accountants and lawyers, in my view, should properly be regarded as the most sophisticated and experienced group of insolvency specialists anywhere in the world. I imagine this would be the subject of some debate on the other side of the Atlantic where there have been other debates raging for many years about which country has the 'better' insolvency and/or bankruptcy system.

I loved my career and made many important friendships in my profession. This modest attempt at opening a window onto my work is one of the ways I am hoping to validate the title I chose for this book. My objectives have excluded upsetting anyone or subverting anything.

There have been and continue to be major delights post-career. They are not limited to free prescriptions, the Freedom pass and the State pension and are despite prostate surgery and radiotherapy. In addition to the joys that three grandsons have brought and the opportunity to rediscover my wife, Wendy, I trained as a Relate Couple Counsellor, passed an audition to become a member of Magic Circle and continue to sit as a Magistrate at Highbury Corner. Until last year I also chaired the City of Westminster sub-committee of The Lord Chancellor's Advisory Committee that interviews candidates for the magistracy.

If you have read this far, I suspect you may enjoy yourself with what follows, which is really all I would like.

**Peter Phillips**
August 2010

# Personalities and Celebrities

'*He was voted "Man of the Year" for 1982*'

*Accountancy* – January 1983

## Personalities and Celebrities

Debt is one of the great levellers.  It does not neglect the apparently wealthy, nor the eminent, nor the famous.  Attitudes to debt have changed over the years and, for example, bankrupts no longer languish in Debtors' prisons.  A number of successful entrepreneurs avow the benefits of the scars they bear from early learning in financial failures.

*'Nothing recedes like success.'*

Walter Winchell, American Journalist

# Hughie Green

In this true (as are all the stories in this book) story, I was introduced, not only to the world of insolvency, but to my late father, Bernard Phillips', advocacy skills.

At about the age of sixteen, I was invited to accompany him to Reading Bankruptcy Court where an application was to be heard on behalf of a Mr Hughie Green. Hughie Green was a Canadian who came to Britain, became a household name in 1955 with the ITV quiz show *Double Your Money* and then went on to host the long running talent show *Opportunity Knocks*.

Mr Green had been made bankrupt as a result of litigation against him which had alleged he had breached his contract with another broadcaster. Creditors had appointed Bernard as his Trustee in Bankruptcy (see glossary).

I have a very clear memory of walking into the Bankruptcy courtroom, the first time I had ever seen such an impressive and authoritative space. In pole position was the Bankruptcy Registrar, who was addressed by counsel on behalf of Mr Green explaining that there was no reasonable prospect of Mr Green's creditors receiving any significant payment for the foreseeable future. Counsel revealed that, fortuitously, a nameless third party was prepared to make sufficient funds available for creditors to receive the equivalent of five shillings in the pound, if Mr Green were able to secure his early discharge from the disabling effects of his Bankruptcy Order.

Bankruptcy legislation over the last few years has made the process far less punitive, and, except in cases where fraud or lack of cooperation by the bankrupt is established, automatic discharge from bankruptcy is granted after a year. Back in the 1960s, however, an individual could remain subject to the rigours of the Bankruptcy Court for a very long time, which encouraged the sort of application that Mr Green was now making.

The Bankruptcy Registrar seemed quite impressed by the offer and invited the representative from the Official Receiver's office (see glossary) to make any observations himself. The Official Receiver's role in the proceedings was to comment on any conduct issues arising out of the bankruptcy. The representative for the Official Receiver also seemed quite content with the proposal and the Bankruptcy Registrar was on the point of delivering his judgement when Bernard, the Trustee, and creditors' representative, respectfully reminded him that one might think it appropriate that he expressed his view as well.

Somewhat chastened, the Registrar invited my father to play his part in the proceedings. At which stage Bernard, with an expression on his face I had grown up to recognise as advance warning of something memorable, eyeballed Hughie Green's advocate and said, 'I regret that the proposal of five shillings in the pound, in my view, is not sufficient. Mr Green will have to double his money'. He sat down amidst uncontainable guffaws and, rather more importantly, went on some months later to distribute ten shillings in the pound, to the creditors. I should for post decimalisation readers confirm that ten shillings in the pound was the equivalent of fifty pence in the pound.

# Life After Debt

Hughie Green was discharged from bankruptcy, moved on to even greater successes and whether despite, or because of, my father's intervention in his financial affairs, even bought him a drink when he bumped into him shortly after his discharge in Wheelers celebrated oyster bar in Old Compton Street in London.

Hughie Green died on 3rd May 1997. After his death it was medically proven that he had been the natural father of Paula Yates, a rumour she had denied when the tabloids first printed the story.

Daily Mail, Saturday, July 8, 1978

# Top designer Gibb faces crisis

THE fashion company behind top designer Bill Gibb is in the hands of a receiver, with debts of £100,000.

Now Gibb, whose creations have adorned the jet-set for a decade, is looking for a new financial backer for the London company, Bill Gibb Ltd.

Among the main creditors is pop tycoon Bryan Morrison, 35, who backed Gibb for five years until they split up in April.

At the time Morrison said the split was for personal reasons but yesterday he revealed that he broke the partnership because of a financial disagreement with Gibb.

Other creditors include the company's 26 staff at the work-room in Kinnly Street, Soho, and at the showroom in Bruton Place, Mayfair. They have not been paid for three weeks. The company also owes more than £10,000 to the Inland Revenue.

Morrison and merchant bankers Hill Samuel, a debenture holder in the company, have appointed chartered accountant Mr Peter Phillips as their receiver.

Yesterday Mr Phillips said : 'I have been put in to keep the busi-

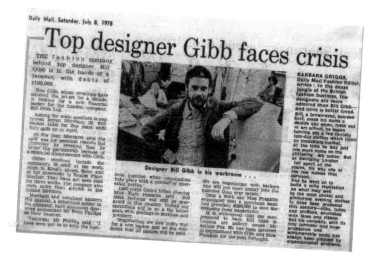

**Designer Bill Gibb in his workroom . . .**

ness together while negotiations take place with a number of interested parties.'

He said that Gibb's fellow director Miss Kate Franklin said : 'Bill Gibb fashions will still be marketed in this country. Indeed our operations will be on a big scale with dealings in perfume and jewellery.

'Negotiations are now under way for a new backer and we are confident that all monies will be held.

BARBARA GRIGGS, Daily Mail Fashion Editor, writes : In the dense jungle of the British fashion business, few designers are more admired than Bill Gibb—and none is better loved.

Gibb, a brown-eyed, bearded Scot, made his name a decade ago when, fresh out of art school, he began turning out a few fantasy late-day clothes which found an immediate market.

At the time he was just one more name on the different arts scene. But as Swinging London calmed, his was one of the few names that survived.

And he went on to build a solid reputation of what may well be the most unreal and glamorous evening clothes to have been produced this century—silks, tulles and chiffons, encrusted with laces and ribbon. But his company, with its tiny turnover and huge production and workmanship costs, has always been plagued by organisational problems.

We are negotiating with backers who will put more money into the business than ever before.'

Only a week ago Miss Franklin announced that a merchant banker had promised £200,000 to save the company from bankruptcy.

It is understood that one man prepared to back Bill Gibb in London art gallery owner Arthur Fox. He has been involved in negotiations with Gibb and Miss Franklin for the past fortnight.

Daily Mail Sun. Album 78

# 'Fairy godfather' puts Bill Gibb back in fashion race

TOP fashion designer Bill Gibb, whose firm has crashed with debts of more than £200,000, has been rescued by a London art gallery owner.

His next spring and summer collections will go ahead as planned, thanks to a deal negotiated with 29-year-old gallery owner Philip Fox.

As a result of the deal, Gibb will also increase his couture collection, introduce a second, less-expensive, ready-to-wear collection and go into the franchise world in a big way.

The ordinary creditors of Bill Gibb Ltd are not so lucky, however. They are unlikely to see a penny of their investment returned.

A creditors' meeting in the West End yesterday was told that total liabilities of the firm stand at £201,936.

The receiver, Mr Peter Phillips, said total assets are unlikely to exceed £100,000. By the time a bank overdraft has been paid off was back tax paid, ordinary creditors owed £112,816 will probably get nothing.

Mr Phillips said that since he was brought into the company a month ago he has tried to make a profit after the 'appalling losses' of previous years.

He has firm orders for goods worth £30,000 to £40,000 on which he hopes to make a profit of around £15,000. He has bought old stock valued at £20,000 into the Bond Street showroom and hopes to make around

**Designer Bill Gibb . . . his spring and summer collections will go ahead**

£10,000 from that.

He has also concluded a deal with Mr Fox's company, Fox Fine Arts, which is buying the goodwill of Bill Gibb for an undisclosed amount.

The creditors' meeting was also told that there are plans to sell the lease of the show-room for £58,000 but as previously there is a dispute over the ownership of the lease.

Gibb was not at the meeting, which was adjourned until October.

The 34-year-old farmer's son whose fortunes in the early 70's rose faster than hemlines was said yesterday to be 'ill and taking a weekend in the country.'

his genius will in future be seen in such diverse things as furs, men's-wear, children's clothes, jewellery, luggage, shoes, cosmetics and perfumery and even linens and towels.

### Promised

Gibb's discoverer, Kate Franklin, who was his business partner in the former company and will be marketing director of the new operation, said : 'It's like a fairy godfather package . . . we have been saved at the 11th hour.

'We have been promised as much capital as we need. It

will probably be around £100,000.

They see Bill's couture collection at the top of the pyramid with the franchising operation next and the ready-to-wear collection. Indeed, without the prestige of the couture collection, the rest of the operation would be of little value.

The ready-to-wear collection will be a range of dresses and coats in the £80 to £120 price range.

News of the new deal was welcomed by the 25 seam-stresses and designers at Gibb's Soho workshop. They claimed they had been unpaid for three weeks.

-16-

## Bill Gibb

In the 1970s, Bill Gibb was one of the world's most celebrated clothing designers. He had established both manufacturing and wholesale businesses.

His relatively limited business experience eventually brought him or rather, a Bryan Morrison, the company's principal funder, to my door. Bryan, himself an extraordinary character, whom I got to know extremely well over the subsequent years, had invested, from his point of view, very significant sums in the Bill Gibb business and had concluded that he could no longer support the losses being made.

He appointed me Receiver and Manager (see glossary) of the Bill Gibb businesses. I took responsibility for running the businesses whilst looking to see if a purchaser could be found for them as going concerns. Whilst there was a lot of initial interest expressed, it seemed to be that proposed purchasers, when they were asked to put money on the table, either did not have the means or the inclination to pay what I thought the business was worth.

I vividly remember one most unpleasant meeting with a father and son negotiating team, who stormed out of an abortive attempt to buy the business from me with the words that have stayed with me ever since, 'Mr Phillips you're just an f***ing pen pusher.'

At a rather more gratifying level, the results of my endeavours enabled me to repay Bryan Morrison's loans in full. As part of

# Couturier comes apart at seams

**Standard Reporter**

BILL GIBB'S hopes of saving his money-troubled couturier company have come apart at the seams.

The former boardroom colleague, polo playing tycoon Bryan Morrison, fell he could not wait any longer for the return of cash advanced to finance the venture.

Chartered accountant Peter Phillips has been appointed receiver like his £161,000 company.

Today, he praised the former talents of a man whose embroidered garments were the world's best dressed, described Kate Franklin's Gibb merchandise that is now selling like a savage bash but getting like a crime.

Not the call for the return of cash by 35-year-old Mr Morrison, a polo art school director of Bill Gibb and a partner in the company, first earlier this year, has filled hopes of preserving the business in its original form.

Debts run into six figures. The most worried creditors are the highly skilled cutters, embroiderers and anones at the Knotty Green, Bucks workshop area (sic) Beroko Palace, Knights, show rooms. They have not been paid for some weeks.

### Trying

Mr Phillips he has also been appointed receiver by another merchant banker, Bill Samuel, as his New Cavendish Street office in Marylebone. "The workers have been told how things stand, I am trying to preserve their jobs by saving the company.

"Bill Gibb's winter collection is available and a number of people are interested in taking over the company as a going concern.

Mr Phillips said it was too early for him to give an opinion on the return for the cash. "I have barely begun my investigation, he said.

The manager of Bill Gibb's workroom in Bond Street said today he was under instruction not to talk about the company and asked what was going on in the workroom.

### Inventory

The staff in the third-floor studio workroom seemed to be taking an inventory of the stock taking the working-out stock collection for Bill Gibb.

The Bill Gibb retail shop in Bond Street is controlled by a separate company and is now under the receiver. Trading there will continue normally.

Bryan Morrison today had his own story about the demise of the company - it need not have gone into the hands of the receiver he said. "Since the receiver put the hands here I have been left holding the baby. Once protection I habit. When asked why he would not again in the fashion business, Morrison said: "I'll have to rook it out."

BILL GIBB—the receiver moves in to his couturier company.

Daily Mail, Wednesday, June 4, 1980.

# Designer Bill Gibb goes bust again

**By BARRY BAKER**

THE Bill Gibb fashion house has collapsed for the second time in two years, with debts of £400,000.

This is twice as much as Gibb, often hailed as Britain's greatest fashion talent, owed two years ago when he was rescued by Mayfair art dealers Alfred and Philip Fox.

After pouring money into the business for no return, the father and son partnership have decided to call a halt.

They have put the company into voluntary liquidation and closed

Mr Gibb's shop in Old Bond Street and workshop in Soho. There will be a creditors' meeting next week.

Scots-born Gibb, 37, rose to fame in the early Seventies. His clients ranged from top fashion setters to prestigious ladies such as Mrs Thatcher and Lady Airey.

In 1974 pop tycoon Bryan Morrison decided to back him and poured thousands of pounds into his business which allowed him time to design dazzling collections.

But four years later Morrison pulled out.

JEAN DODSON, Daily Mail Fashion and Style Editor writes: At a time when many established designers are finding the going tough, the question of all the trade asks today is can this be another example of the Bill Gibb bad luck jinx, or is it downright bad management?

His flamboyant dresses were bought by stylish actresses such as Lalla Ward and Elaine Stritch. But many of his clothes were more like works of art than fashions for the working woman.

the business disposal process a huge quantity of Bill Gibb's wonderful vintage gowns were sold at a televised auction.

After this experience Bryan told me he would never involve himself in the gown trade again, which seems to have been a wise decision, as he spent many years enjoying the yield of his investment in BeeGee Music Rights, as well as his involvement in Wham!, the immensely successful duo that included George Michael.

Although I did not see Bryan for several years, I had noted his regularly appearances in *The Sunday Times'* Rich List. Very sadly, I read his obituary in *The Times* following his death in October 2008 after an accident playing polo.

# NIGEL Dempster

Daily Mail, Friday, January 9, 1998

# Tale of the old school T-shirt

**Party to some inside info: Gerald, with wife Gail**

■ HERON Corporation boss Gerald Ronson did a double-take when he saw a fellow guest walk in to breakfast at the Sandy Lane Hotel in Barbados, where he has been holidaying with his wife Gail.

The chap was dressed in a T-shirt bearing the legend 'HM Prison Ford' — a reminder of the standard-issue clothing Ronson wore when he did six months inside for his part in the Guinness scandal.

While other guests looked on with interest to see how the potentially embarrassing situation would develop, Ronson (who became something of a hero during his time at Ford, running business courses for inmates) walked over and asked: 'Are you qualified to wear that shirt?'

When the man looked bemused, Ronson went on: 'I mean, did you have a little stay at Ford?' It turned out the chap had never been detained at Her Majesty's pleasure; he was simply the son of one of Ford's prison visitors.

Ronson tells me: 'Some of the other guests thought the T-shirt was in bad taste, but it didn't bother me. He was a very nice young man and he told me that one of the people his mother visited was Ernest Saunders.'

*Daily Mail* – 9th January 1971

## Appearances can be Deceptive

This particular story might be referred to as a *cross-over* tale in that it does not come, strictly speaking, from my career; nevertheless some ironies may be observed in it.

Bernard's widow, Lilian, (now Lilian Holdsworth MBE), amongst her many accomplishments, became a member of the then Board of Visitors (now the Independent Monitoring Board) looking after the administration at Ford Open Prison. Some years ago, for a Christmas present, she gave me a t-shirt made in the prison. It was a very nice looking t-shirt, in navy blue, bearing a portcullis motif and the words 'HM Prison Ford' on the front.

Wendy (my wonderful, long suffering and only wife) and I had decided to take a well-earned break just after Christmas in Barbados. I decided, being pale and exhausted, to wear the Christmas present on the first morning of our holiday and so strolled down to the breakfast buffet suitably adorned.

As I was toying with the grapefruit segments a shadow fell over me and a voice boomed, 'Are you qualified to wear that t-shirt?'

I looked round and into the eyes of someone whose face I thought I recognised, but seeing no point in beating around the bush, said, 'No, I'm not qualified to wear this t-shirt, it was a Christmas present.'

My new acquaintance looked at me cynically and said, 'Well that means I'm the only one in this hotel qualified to wear that t-shirt, how do you do, I'm Gerald Ronson!'

# Life After Debt

My comprehensive demonstration of total embarrassment was clearly convincing as he seemed quite sympathetic to my explanation of how I was wearing the t-shirt and that I had had no intention of embarrassing him or anyone else in the hotel. To my surprise he thought the incident was extremely amusing and took me over to his table of breakfast guests and colleagues including Philip Green, now Sir Philip Green, and Robert Earl (of Planet Hollywood) who far from seeing the funny side of the encounter looked ready to re-arrange my physiognomy.

Very much to Gerald Ronson's credit he insisted that he thought the matter to be highly entertaining and calmed them down.

It also seemed pretty obvious who may have contacted the late Nigel Dempster at the *Daily Mail* to give them the story which appeared on the beaches of the hotel later that week.

My anonymity has been totally preserved until now!

## Doctor Heal Thyself

This is a truly sad story with alarming elements.

In the 1960s the public's imagination was regularly captured by the feats of endurance and stamina performed by a lady called Dr Barbara Moore.  Although my memory now is not good enough to remember the purpose of her very long walks, including one from Land's End to John O'Groats, and the web seems to be almost empty of any information about her, I clearly remember her being well regarded as a strong-willed eccentric.

This is the small amount of information that Wikipedia discloses about Barbara Moore.

> Dr Barbara Moore (22 December 1903 – 14 May 1977) was a Russian-born health enthusiast who gained celebrity in the early 1960s for her long-distance walking.
>
> In December 1959 she walked from Edinburgh to London. In early 1960 she walked from John O'Groats to Land's End in 23 days.  She then undertook an 85-day, 3,387 mile walk from San Francisco to New York City, where she arrived on July 6, 1960.
>
> She was a vegetarian and reputed to be a breatharian.  She walked with only nuts, honey, raw fruit and vegetable juice for nourishment.
>
> She died in a London hospital on 14 May 1977.
>
> Her John O'Groats to Land's End walk caught the attention of Harry Griffin who advocated a revival of the Bob Graham Round as possibly a much sterner test of fitness.

# Life After Debt

For reasons that I cannot now bring to mind, she was made bankrupt and Bernard was appointed her Trustee. The emotional pressures of the circumstances leading to her bankruptcy as well as the publicity attached to it doubtless had a profound influence on her stability and she became a recluse in the house that required to be sold on behalf of her creditors.

Bernard on a number of occasions tried to arrange an appointment to visit her to discuss, in a civilised way, how best to proceed, but on the one occasion that he did indicate he was going to call upon her, she warned him off by explaining she would be waiting for him with a shotgun!

Discretion, as usual, was the better part of Dad's valour; no shots were ever fired and matters were concluded civilly.

## Miss Whiplash and the Pink Range Rover

In 1992 Lee Manning, one of my then partners and a specialist in handling football club failures, was together with me, appointed Joint Receiver and Manager of Armitage and Walker Ltd.

Armitage and Walker was a well known London car showroom and service & repair depot. When receivers are appointed to any business their overriding hope is to preserve that business. What also often accompanies this challenge is a legal responsibility to protect any third party property in the possession of the insolvent business. In this case, unsurprisingly, we found ourselves being bombarded with enquiries from people who had brought their cars in for service and, at the point of the company's collapse, were awaiting the collection or return of their vehicles.

The unravelling of these situations is not normally very much more than the tedious exercise of locating the vehicle, locating the owner and exchanging the vehicle for a payment for the outstanding work. However, on this occasion one particular vehicle's owner created quite a stir.

In the care of Armitage and Walker at the time of its collapse, was a pink Range Rover owned by a Lindi St Clair who was also known as Miss Whiplash after being publicly described as a prostitute and a lesbian. Miss St Clair had also entered into two marriages of convenience in 1995 and 1999. She achieved additional recognition when she accused the Inland Revenue of trying to live off immoral earnings when they asked her to pay income tax, they having classified prostitution as a trade.

Lindi St Clair stood for Parliament eleven times

# Life After Debt

Miss St Clair, on discovering that Armitage and Walker was in the hands of receivers, sent a spirited fax to our offices demanding the release of the pink Range Rover to her without delay. She supplied a list of the contents of the vehicle, which she also expected to find intact.

What she listed as the contents of the car was detailed in *The Independent* for Thursday, 22nd October 1992.

> These include 100 hard-core sex magazines, 10 pairs of police handcuffs, 10 pairs of leg irons, 1,000 condoms, a leather strait-jacket and a body bag. Lee Manning of Buchler Phillips says the receivers are diligently searching for the items among the company's stock.

Happily Miss St Clair was satisfied with what was returned to her with the minimum possible delay by the receivers.

# All In A Day's Work

"You'll soon find you get hardened to this job, Hargreaves."

## All in a Day's Work

When I read the first draft of these tales, apart from enjoying them, I obtained not a little pleasure from reminding myself that the cliché image of the accountant as a boring number cruncher seems to have had no relationship to my own experience.

I sense that my former professional colleagues and competitors would feel just the same way about their own careers.

*'A bargain is something you can't use at a price you can't resist.'*

Franklin P. Jones, American businessman or humorist.  Who he actually was is unclear.

'No refunds, but I can let you have two
front row seats for the Bankruptcy Court!'

*Daily Mail* – 10th September 1991
Mahood

## Liquidator

The name Keith Prowse has been associated for decades with the arrangement of travel and sporting events. It is currently described as the UK's largest independent ticket agency.

Its ownership however has changed over the years along with that of many other well known brands that have survived earlier critical financial challenges, with the help of the insolvency profession. In the early 1980s the development capital group that had been funding the Keith Prowse Group called me in, as they had concluded they could not continue to provide support to the loss-making companies. I was asked to take on the task of liquidating the companies' assets which entailed calling meetings of creditors (see glossary) and assisting the directors in preparing their Statements of Affairs (see glossary) for each of the Group companies.

One of the companies ran the Keith Prowse office in New York, which I was required to visit and assess before creditors met at their meetings to be held in London. I was therefore given the opportunity to pay my first visit to New York and indeed to the USA. The urgent nature of the work that was required to be carried out by me in time for the meeting led those who had asked me to help to dispatch me on Concorde!

It was therefore a very excited me that arrived at the desk of a very surly immigration officer, early in the US morning itching to get on with the days challenges. The officer was clearly interested in the sorts of candidates for admission disgorged from Concorde and quizzed me at some length.

*Accountancy Age* - 1989

# Life After Debt

All was going well until he asked me what I did for a living, to which I quite honestly and maybe a little insensitively offered 'I'm a Liquidator'. There was most definitely a sharp intake of breath and he asked me to repeat my answer, which I did somewhat apologetically.

He said, 'Wait there', and stormed off. He swiftly returned accompanied by two colleagues and asked me to repeat my answer to them. I complied.

My heart was starting to simultaneously accelerate and sink when one of the new interviewing panel snapped at me, 'Do you liquidate people?' I found that question quite easy to answer and said 'Of course not, I liquidate companies'.

At this my original welcoming Mr Surly smiled at me and said, 'Good, here we liquidate people. Welcome to New York, Mr Phillips'.

I stumbled through to a taxi and to a day's hard work, sensing that one day I would want to share that story with a lot of people.

An interesting postscript to the Keith Prowse Group liquidation was that in the course of reviewing the arrangements between the Group and its financiers I uncovered an indemnity in the accounts given by the development capital organisation, which meant that I was able to open all the meetings of creditors which had attracted many angry people by telling them that they would all be paid in full, which they were.

## Lebanese International Airlines

Barely a day passes without a reminder of tensions, hostilities and suffering in the Middle East.

The year in which I qualified as a Chartered Accountant, 1968, was the year in which Israeli commandoes blew up thirteen airliners at Beirut airport in reprisal for an attack in Athens by Lebanese trained Palestinian guerrillas.

The airline company was sued for rent arrears on its London premises and forced into Compulsory Liquidation under the supervision of the Court (see glossary). At a meeting of creditors held in London, Bernard was appointed Liquidator and on his behalf I contacted the company's managing director, in order to explain to him the Liquidator's obligations and requirements. The director came to our offices and unsurprisingly was not at all happy at the chain of events that led him there. The atmosphere was further charged by his understanding that both the Liquidator and myself were Jewish.

Our brief, on behalf of creditors was of course to identify, secure and realise any assets for their benefit.

The director indicated that apart from the wreckage of the thirteen planes at Beirut airport the only asset, aside from a nominal amount of office furniture and fittings in the London office, was an ageing Bristol Britannia aircraft that had somehow survived the Israeli attack. I explained that, of course, I would have to take steps to have the aircraft valued with a view to realising such worth in the liquidation, and that I planned to instruct specialist valuers to visit Beirut airport.

He was distinctly unimpressed, advised me that no assistance would be afforded to my agents and that they would not be allowed access to the aircraft. I therefore suggested that one of my managers could accompany the auctioneers, if that would help. It was clear that that made absolutely no difference to his willingness to cooperate.

I finally suggested that I would be prepared to visit the airport myself on behalf of the Liquidator to which he responded, 'Mr Phillips if you come to Beirut, you will not come home'. As I seem to recall I decided to send my valuers, who did come home but not with very good news for the creditors, as the Bristol Britannia in terms of realisability was a liability rather than an asset.

*'Married women never get ulcers. But they are carriers!'*

*Financial Times* – 5th June 1990
Cummings

## Breeches and British & Commonwealth plc

In May 1990 British & Commonwealth Holdings plc was placed
into Administration (see glossary), and with debts of £2 billion,
that company then became by far and away the largest ever
corporate insolvency in the United Kingdom. Here are two
stories from the twenty-four hours leading up to the moment
of Administration that made this a bizarre weekend.

It was Saturday evening at about 7.00 pm, I was leaving the
house with Wendy to join some friends for dinner when the
telephone rang. We were running late and my wife was not
impressed with my returning to see who was calling.

At the other end of the line was Stephen Adamson (now CBE)
then Senior Partner of the Insolvency Division of Ernst & Young,
and who had taken on the Presidency of the Insolvency
Practitioners Association after myself in 1989. He and I, and his
and my firms knew and respected each other very well and the
purpose of his call was to ask whether I would be prepared to
act, with him, as Joint Administrator of British &
Commonwealth.

His firm had been assisting the company in preparing its
application for Administration, and had concluded that they
required someone from outside their firm to independently
pursue some major litigation against a UK clearing bank of
which Ernst & Young was the auditor. I could hardly believe this
conversation was taking place, as at that time in my career I
had only been running my firm Buchler Phillips for a year and a
half, and the opportunity to become involved in an assignment
such as this was quite frankly unbelievable. It took me about

point one of a second to make it clear that I should be delighted to help and I enquired what the next step might be.

Stephen explained that an application was going to be made to a Judge in Chambers (see glossary) on the following evening and therefore could I attend a planning meeting at Ernst & Young's offices early the following morning. Still not believing this conversation was really taking place and being increasingly aware of an increasingly impatient Mrs Phillips at my elbow I tried to negotiate a meeting later in the day, but was told that an early morning meeting was essential.

Stephen did not know, and I assume to this day, frankly was not very impressed when I explained that I had for many years exercised horses in Richmond Park early on Sunday mornings. With characteristic humour and tolerance Stephen gently convinced me that maybe I could come to the very early morning meeting and then go off riding. I will never forget the various expressions around the boardroom table of lawyers, merchant bankers and accountants when yours truly strolled in wearing breeches and full length riding boots on that late spring Sunday morning.

Later that day, as planned, the professional contingent, including me, now more appropriately clad, arrived at the Judge's house where we were led upstairs by his wife to find the Judge lying in bed wearing a burgundy smoking jacket. Sufficient chairs and two lecterns had been placed at the foot of his bed for the participants and their advocates to talk to His Lordship.

*The Independent* – 5th June 1990

# Montagu must pay record £172m to B&C

by Joanne Hart

MERCHANT bank Samuel Montagu was today ordered to pay a record £172 million in damages and interest to British & Commonwealth, the collapsed financial services group formerly headed by John Gunn.

The High Court award is the biggest made against a British merchant bank. It revolves around advice given by Samuel Montagu in connection with the ability of finance boutique Quadrex to pay B&C money for a deal struck in 1987.

Samuel Montagu said it would appeal against the court decision. In the meantime though, it is paying the cash straight to the creditors of B&C, which went into administration with debts of £1 billion.

Administrator Peter Phillips of Buchler Phillips said: "The sum improves the recovery for B&C creditors by up to 18p in the pound. It represents a dramatic enhancement of their realisations to date and potential dividends."

"Even though Samuel Montagu is appealing, the cash will be in our hands and earning interest of some £10 million a year.

The figure payable is split between £101 million in damages and £71 million in interest. Quadrex is asked to pay separate damages of about £10 million. Samuel Montagu is expected to

B&C's Gunn, left, Montagu's McIntosh, centre, and Klesch of Quadrex

have to pay up to £8 million more after a short hearing in December.

Montagu's parent company, HSBC Holdings — which took over Midland Bank and Samuel Montagu last July — is making a provision of £85 million in respect of the judgment though it expects the ruling to be reversed on appeal.

Mr Justice Gatehouse found in 1991 that Samuel Montagu and Quadrex were liable for damages but the decision on the amount was postponed until today. The

case goes back to 1987 when Quadrex and B&C were both stalking fund manager and money broker Mercantile House. B&C knew it had to dispose of parts of Mercantile for its deal to be financially viable and agreed to sell the wholesale broking division for £280 million to Quadrex under the assurance from Samuel Montagu that Quadrex had enough money to pay for the business.

In May 1991, Mr Justice Gatehouse ruled that Quadrex was in breach of contract for failing to complete the purchase of the broking division.

He also held that Ian McIntosh, then head of corporate finance at Samuel Montagu and now deputy chairman, knowingly and negligently took a risk.

*Evening Standard* – 18th October 1993

# Life After Debt

The Judge explained that he had recently suffered a back injury and that whilst he was perfectly comfortable in the position in which we found him, cautioned us against anything happening that might require him to move. Movement would undoubtedly occasion him severe pain and that that might have a negative impact on the progress of the application.

London professionals being what they are, no pain was occasioned to the Judge, the application was granted and Stephen Adamson and I became Joint Administrators of British & Commonwealth Holdings.

I successfully concluded litigation against the clearing bank recovering £170 million for the creditors. The creditors of the British & Commonwealth Group have been paid back the vast majority of their claims.

This picture was taken outside court, after victory against Samuel Montagu. I am on the left of Nick Stadlen QC and John Gunn, the former Chairman of British and Commonwealth is in the right foreground.

It appeared opposite this advert, for Samuel Montagu's parent: the Midland Bank.

## Timing is Everything

My principal function, as Joint Administrator of British &
Commonwealth, was to take control of litigation that had just
been commenced by the company, against a number of parties
claiming sums, in the early 1990s, approaching £200 million.
One of the defendants was Samuel Montagu, an extremely well
respected merchant bank, and a subsidiary of the then Midland
Bank.  The heavyweight financial press assiduously followed the
litigation, which eventually was settled between the Court of
Appeal and the House of Lords by the payment to me by Samuel
Montagu of £170 million, which, at the time, was the largest
litigation settlement ever recorded in the United Kingdom.

I don't know how many other readers of the *Evening Standard*
on the day in question spotted the exquisite irony of the
juxtaposition of a report on this litigation with the
advertisement placed by Midland Bank, a copy of which appears
on the facing page.

DAILY EXPRESS Friday November 5 1971

# Sex shop crashes

### Good start... then £87,000 loss after post strike hit sales

**By CHRISTOPHER WHITE**

Ann: 'I can't wait to start a business again'

ANN SUMMERS, the one-time secretary who launched Britain's first sex shop, heard yesterday how the company had gone bust.

A £232,000 turnover ended with a loss of £87,000.

Miss Summers, aged 30, lent her name to the company that opened the controversial sex-aids shop in London's Edgware Road in September 1970.

She quit last May—and three months later began court proceedings to stop Ann Summers Ltd., from using her name.

## HALF A SHARE

Miss Summers still holds half a share, owned jointly with Bradrose Ltd., who issued £2,000 worth of shares when the company was launched by Mr. Michael Waterfield.

Standing at the back of a creditors' meeting yesterday with her fiance, 41-year-old public relations consultant Mr. David Jones, Miss Summers heard of high wages and consultants' fees that turned a £232,000 turnover into £64,146 worth of debts.

Mr. Bernard Phillips, who was appointed as liquidator by the creditors, spoke of "wages, salaries, and fees out of all proportion to what should have been paid." Mr. Waterfield was one of the consultants paid a total of £21,000.

## COSTS

Wages from the time the company began trading until its closure less than two years later amounted to £48,000. Advertising and printing costs amounting to £27,000.

Summing up the company's history, Mr. Phillips said: "It had a fairly important opening stage, and a disastrous middle stage owing to the postal strike and extraordinary overheads.

"Various aspects of still have to be looked into," he added.

"Gross profits over the trading period were £97,527."

Miss Summers said later: "I don't say I am the most qualified person, but I enjoy helping people with their sex problems and I can't wait to start a business again."

*Daily Express* – 5th November 1971

## Ann Summers

For those of you turning to this story in search of salacious material, I regret you are going to be disappointed, but I think you will find it interesting for other reasons.

The name Ann Summers, of course, is now extremely well established, but I imagine that few people realise that the name Ann Summers was the name of the PA to the original Chairman of the company that bore her name. The then Chairman's name was also one to conjour with ... 'Dandy' Kim Waterfield.

I first met Ms Ann Summers when as Company Secretary she was recommended to consult Bernard.

The business was operated from three retail outlets including two in London and Ann Summers was accompanied by two brothers, Ralph and David Gold, who were very interested in acquiring the business as a going concern from its ultimate Liquidator.

The company was in serious financial difficulties. I was in my late twenties and a little intrigued to see how my father would deal with obtaining the sort of information about the company's business that he would need to share with creditors at the inevitable creditors' liquidation meeting. He was provided with voluminous and detailed lists of the company's stocks and he leafed through it apparently oblivious as to the true nature of the enterprise.

He paused at one stage and asked, 'I see you have 3000 cans of Love Foam, what is Love Foam?'

# Life After Debt

One of the Gold brothers, looking quite embarrassed and who had evidently seen Dad as an elegant sixty-year old chartered accountant volunteered, 'It comes in cans'.

Bernard pursued his enquiries with, 'But what is it?'

The hesitant response was, 'It comes in eight flavours'. Everyone in the room, except Bernard, was cringing. He pressed on, 'But what do you do with it?'

A long pause ended with one of the brothers Gold admitting 'You spray it on the one you love....'

The inevitable further pressure from Bernard, 'and then...?' an even longer pause and gulp for air with yours truly wishing he was in another room in another place at another time.

Then came the final admission, 'You lick it off'.

I should like to say that that was the end of the interrogation but Bernard then moved onto asking for a better understanding of stock of 15,000 *Go Go* tablets!

I have often wondered since that time what my father's memories of that meeting might be, but sadly I never had the nerve to ask him.

A couple of postscripts; the company proceeded into liquidation, Bernard was appointed its Liquidator and with the agreement of the creditors the Gold brothers bought the business assets of Ann Summers. That business, in its massively enhanced form, is now managed by Jacqueline Gold. She is the daughter of one of the brothers.

A more sobering encounter took place shortly after the liquidation started, when a senior representative of the Department of Health came to see me about concerns they had over the safety of some of the earlier lines carried by the original company. He revealed that they were considering commencing proceedings against directors of the original company who might be regarded as responsible. The only director was unavailable and the only other officer, the lady who gave her name to the company, had had no managerial responsibilities.

To the best of my knowledge no proceedings were ever put in train.

## British Glandular Products

This is a very short tale, about a very small company, that had a very brief existence supplying hormone tablets by mail order.

I think, a little like the difficulties referred to in the Ann Summers story, pressures from authorities and certain anxieties within the customer base forced the company into liquidation, with very few remaining assets.

I agreed to handle the liquidation for the creditors in the hope that the few remaining assets would fund the costs of doing the required work.

This turned out to be a bad decision, as for a couple of years after the liquidation started I was besieged by customers, who were either dissatisfied with what they had bought, or unsatisfied in the sense that they had sent money in for products which had not been delivered to them.

Dealing sensitively and courteously with these issues made this assignment, to put it mildly, uncommercial, but it wound up a successful candidate for this collection of anecdotes.

If you are further interested in this company, their literature is in the special collections at Sussex University Library.

## Too Clever by Half

Personal bankruptcy can be a devastating experience for not only the debtor but his or her spouse and family.

Some decades ago however when there was still the illusion amongst some potential bankrupts that putting their house in the name of their spouse would protect it from their creditors it fell to us to deal with the affairs of an extraordinary individual.

In the first place, he was a titled gentleman whom I will not name, but the unique aspect of his case was that in the course of investigating his affairs it was discovered that he had committed bigamy. The discovery followed unsurprisingly from claims to two properties that he owned from two wives with different names! Needless to say the claims of both apparent wives were defeated but that was perhaps the least of that titled gentleman's then impending problems.

*The Times* – February 1982
Marc

## The Bath Club, London

The Bath Club London was one of London's longest established and best regarded gentlemen's clubs. However, in the 1970s the Department of Health unfortunately concluded that it also possessed some of London's oldest kitchen equipment. It required the Club to re-equip its kitchens, or else.

When the estimated costs were put before the management committee it became clear that the matter would have to be put to the membership.

The choices would be stark: either to inject further capital to upgrade the catering facilities or to close the Club.

The Chairman of the Club consulted our firm and we guided the committee through the tortuous process of consultation.

The unique and bizarre challenge at the time was the distinction between Members and *Members*. On the one hand there were Club Members who had paid their subscriptions and on the other hand, there were statutory shareholder Members.

Procedurally speaking, the only Members that could be consulted on the options were the statutory Members, the Shareholders.

During the consultation period it became clear that the property development value of the Club's site was likely to be significant and, unsurprisingly, the shareholder members of the Club made it clear that they were much more interested in realising their investment than providing further finance.

# Life After Debt

As might also have been expected, the subscribing Members, that were not necessarily the same as the Shareholders, felt differently.

This resulted in a number of very difficult meetings and the final conclusion that the Club would close.

In the 1970s the newspapers were full of reports of workers strikes, sit-ins and other industrial actions – but the Bath Club membership took this art to an entirely new level when on the day of the planned closure, a number of elderly members, some even in wheelchairs, refused to leave their much loved Club. Statesmanlike handling on the night surmounted this hurdle, the Club was redeveloped and one class of member did very well indeed.

## How to Handle Yourself in Sicily

Over the decades I have noticed that failing travel companies tend to announce their collapse in the early autumn of any year. This has been explained to me as the natural consequence of the drying up of cash flow after the summer holidays, and meeting head-on the cash requirement for brochures etc for the following seasons.

One of the more interesting travel organisations I became involved with was the Discovering group of companies, which were extremely popular with Italians in the UK wishing, either to go home for holidays, or to simply visit the extraordinary island of Sicily. The company's operations were largely funded by a Sicilian tourist grant for each person it transported there.

One of the problems of dealing with a travel company failure at the initial stages is how to address the challenges of holiday makers stranded wherever they might be or of holiday makers who have pre-paid for their holidays. Working alongside my father we were able to secure the sale of the goodwill and assets of the Group, protecting all these open positions.

By far the most testing part of this assignment was when it came to recovering the significant arrears of Sicilian tourist grants which, in the 1970s, totalled some hundreds of thousands of pounds.

Bernard generously volunteered me to visit Palermo just before Christmas one year to meet the representatives of the Sicilian Tourist Grant Association. Sicily in December is not a sunny welcoming environment and neither, it seemed, was the office of the gentleman I had to visit.

I explained the purpose of my visit and he sat back and took a long look at me, leaned back and opened the doors to some very large cupboards right behind him.  These were full of box files with names on their spines. (Readers will note the absence of computer records, as a result of computers then requiring invention for ordinary businesses and people). I could see Horizon Holidays, Courtline Holidays and other then household names from the graveyard of many previous years in the travel industry.

The official looked at me with what might have been a benign way, or the very opposite, but what he said made its desired impact.  'Mr Phillips, I would respectfully urge you to deal with the processing of these claims with me in a civilised manner or you will find your claim in this cupboard, alongside the claims of those other Liquidators and Receivers, many years after they were put in, who found it rather too difficult to behave in a way I suggest you consider.'

I really had no inclination to ask what had gone wrong with the other companies' claims and just pressed on, in what turned out to be something he seemingly regarded as an acceptable manner.

Probably six or seven months later Bernard was invited to attend the same office in Palermo, by which time the climate was much more inviting, not merely economically.

# Life After Debt

When it was clear that the tourist grant was about to be released, Bernard turned up for his meeting, was welcomed warmly but was then told to identify himself. He produced his passport but was told by the kind gentleman I had met the previous Christmas that that was not good enough!

On enquiring what might be acceptable he was told he had to have his identity verified by two Sicilian residents who would be prepared to confirm, in writing, that they had known him for two years.

Somewhat bemused, Bernard left the office, with the hour he had been granted to meet these interesting requirements and sat down for a coffee with the local solicitor whose services he had retained.

The solicitor was not at all worried, saying, 'Just give me a moment' and a moment or so later, appeared with two individuals whom he introduced to Bernard as being the car park attendant at the Sicilian Tourist Grant office and a young lady who was the chair of the local Communist party.

Both readily agreed to attest to Bernard's identity in writing. My father did not enquire how their enthusiastic cooperation had been secured at such short notice. The two individuals and their statements were placed before the official at the Sicilian Tourist Grant office. No one's, save perhaps Bernard's, eyelids flickered in the slightest, the claim was accepted and a few weeks later a lot of Lira (then the Italian currency) were remitted to the United Kingdom for the group's creditors.

## The Biter Bit

Many years ago I discovered Charles Tyrwhitt the mail-order shirt company. I liked what they sold and I liked the way they did it. Not surprisingly I became and remain a regular customer.

It was an important lesson for me the day I received through the post a letter informing me that Receivers and Managers had been appointed to the company and that whilst they acknowledged that I had sent a payment in advance for my *unsecured* (see glossary). In due course, when the company proceeded from receivership (see glossary) into liquidation (see glossary) and if there were any funds remaining, after paying off the banks secured lending, they would be distributed equally between all the creditors of whom I was one.

My distress was much more the fear that I would never see the shirts I had ordered and that the company would sink without trace rather than the relatively modest financial loss I might inevitably suffer.

The really sobering part of the letter was that one of the two Receivers who had signed it was me!

Sadly, at that particular time, so many businesses were collapsing, and cases were being taken on in such large numbers that when one was acting as support Receiver, as I was in the Charles Tyrwhitt case, day-to-day conduct was handled by another partner as **lead** Receiver. I shocked myself by realising that, as I had signed off my part of the letter to creditors it had not even registered that I was going to be one of them!

# Life After Debt

A very happy postscript to this story is that we were able to find a purchaser for the business as a going concern. This business has, to use a knackered cliché, gone from strength to strength certainly for reasons far more important than my continuing custom which they still enjoy.

*'Luck is getting a kidney transplant from a chronic bed wetter.'*

## Now you see it, now you don't

Banks usually get an extremely bad press about their allegedly aggressive attitude towards struggling borrowers.

From my experience, this is not always fair.

Sometime back I found myself asked by an extremely highly regarded private bank to assist them in making a decision as to whether or not to continue to support a retail antiques business near Windsor.

The directors of the company agreed to allow me to meet with them and to review the company's position.  The company had borrowed a considerable sum of money from the private bank to acquire an impressive stock of antiques of which the directors seemed extremely proud.

The business challenge was that very few people were buying any of the antiques, whilst at the same time interest was clocking up on the overdraft.

At the time it seemed to me that urgent action needed to be taken by the bank, which could have included requiring the directors to provide their personal guarantees for any further borrowing and a planned reduction of stock levels through a sale.  These and other recommendations were put by me in my formal reports to the company and the bank.

I heard nothing more from anybody for the better part of a year. What I did hear next was the embarrassed voice of the senior bank executive who had originally sought my assistance to say that, far from putting any pressure on their customer, matters had been allowed to continue as before until an attempt had been made to pay a visit to the antique shop by the bank. The bank then discovered that the shop was empty and closed. The directors (and presumably the stock) had left the country!

The bank was so shaken by this experience it introduced it as a case study in subsequent internal training.

## Long Firm Fraud - two Dogs, the Old Bailey and the IRA

Early in my career I was dealing with the liquidation of a group of companies that appeared to have been used to carry out, what was known as in professional circles, as a long firm fraud. This term of art was used simply to describe the process of establishing an apparently *bona fide* trading business and gaining the confidence of its suppliers such that, without warning, massively larger credit than previously tolerated would be obtained from all suppliers simultaneously. The goods supplied on such enhanced credit, moved to another company, were sold on and then the group of companies would collapse, leaving enormous debts and limited assets.

Liquidators having been appointed and quickly realising what had happened, an initial challenge was to secure the remaining stock of the companies in their warehouse in the East End of London.

We decided, after discussion, to install security guards with a dog but were amused to receive a telephone call from the security company to say they could not obtain access to the premises because there was a dog already in it. A suspect director had thought he could head off our accessing the books and papers of the company in this way, but the security company advised us, put at its simplest, that *their dog was bigger than his* and we allowed them to take control.

This was achieved without any blood being shed, either of the human or canine variety.

# Life After Debt

After detailed investigation a report was made by my firm to the appropriate authorities about the evident fraud and, after what seemed an eternity, a Detective Inspector called upon us to say that he had been assigned the responsibility of pursuing the matter to trial.

We enquired as to whether he was familiar with company fraud matters and were troubled to hear him answer, 'No this is my first fraud matter, I have been on the murder squad for twenty years'.

When the matter came to trial, on its opening day at the Old Bailey the appalling IRA bombing atrocity took place, injuring a number of members of both the public and the legal fraternities. The trial eventually resumed and I was called to give evidence of my findings. I spent a draining three days in the witness box being cross-examined by the two defendants' counsel, Messrs Greville Janner and Ivor Richard, both of whom subsequently became MPs. At the end of a very long trial the two directors were found guilty and imprisoned.

## Timing can be Everything

In the early, slightly uninformed, days of banks appointing Receivers to businesses, not all banks always warned companies that Receivers were about to knock on their front doors.

This was particularly unfortunate in the case of a marvellous gentleman, Mr Hylton Lacey, whose company, Profile Publications, was put into my care, as its Receiver and Manager.

I arrived at the head office of Profile Publications one morning unannounced and was taken to Mr Lacey's office, where I introduced myself and my new found responsibilities. The start of an extremely good friendship was disturbingly prefaced by his telling me that I had arrived on the morning of his fiftieth birthday.

The company which had, in former years, become highly respected for its superior aircraft and defence system publications was essentially a first class business which Hylton Lacey had allowed to lose pace and focus, whilst he had been thinking he was enjoying the fruits of his successes relaxing in Bermuda.

Very much to his credit he re-established himself in the UK and Europe, and largely thanks to his extraordinary commitment assisted me in, for the only time in my career, after three years, withdrawing from the receivership having dealt with all creditors and returning the company into its original ownership, namely that of Hylton Lacey esquire.

It was with great sadness I heard many years later that he had passed away.  He taught me a number of lessons about dignity, loyalty and commitment.

**Experience** – *'If you think experience is expensive, try ignorance.'*

## School's Out

Many years ago I was appointed Liquidator of a long established school for young ladies, near Great Missenden, a little north of London, called the Hamden House School for Girls. I was consulted in the middle of the summer term after the Health & Safety Authorities had warned the school that unless it replaced its kitchens they would close them down.

The school simply did not have the funds to comply with these requirements and asked me to deal with the formalities of liquidation. As I familiarised myself with the school's obligations I realised that the end of year speech day, which I was going to have to be cancel, was likely to have a notable speaker committed to attend. I enquired who that might be. I could hardly believe my ears to be told that the speaker that had agreed to present the prizes was Sir Kenneth Cork, the author of the Cork Report on Insolvency law reform and someone of whom I made significant mention in the introduction to this book.

I dropped a personal note to Sir Kenneth, which was arguably tongue in cheek, explaining the position and sadly cancelling the arrangements that had been made with him, but also inviting him to let me have a note of any claim he might have in the liquidation which would, of course, be treated as an unsecured claim.

To say I got a terse response would to not do justice to what I really did receive but I can't really say I was surprised.

## Going out with a Bang

In the early 1980s I was appointed Receiver and Manager of a long established company, Ronson Ltd, which had, most famously, established the international cigarette lighter brand. This company had no connection with Mr Gerald Ronson, referred to earlier in this book.

The bank that appointed me was owed several million pounds and general concern was being expressed about the conduct of the then Chairman of the company. As was normal, it was my intention to present myself at the company's head office and talk through the options with the Chairman.

I sensed things were going to be slightly out of the ordinary when I was told that the Chairman was in apparent permanent residence at the Grosvenor House Hotel in London.

I together with my Joint Receiver directed ourselves to Park Lane and up to the door of the suite in which we were told Mr X resided. I rang the doorbell which was opened by a very attractive young lady in an extremely short dress. I asked to speak to Mr X but was told he was unavailable. It took some considerable pressure and the revelation of the purpose of the visit for the young lady to scamper away and, a few minutes later, be replaced by the man whom I needed to see. He was in a towelling robe eating a large bowl of vanilla ice cream, which he subsequently told me represented his then strict diet.

I and my Joint Receiver were invited in and we sat down with Mr X and a number of other gentlemen who appeared to be in one shape or form looking after him. What started off as a relatively civilised conversation soon descended into something far less pleasant.

With great difficulty we proceeded to get on with the task that had been set us and a short time afterwards Mr X fled the country. The assignment lasted a number of years. We sold the business and repaid the bank in full.

To the best of my knowledge the Ronson brand still survives.

## The Power of Suggestion

Some years ago, I was telephoned by a firm of solicitors who were representing an individual who had been injured using one of the moving pavements at London's Heathrow airport. The ensuing litigation resulted in a judgement against an international airline, on the basis that it was the airline that had carried the injured passenger that bore responsibility for injuries deplaning.

The partner at the firm of solicitors that contacted me had tried every conventional route to persuade the respected international airline to pay the damages that had been awarded by the Court and had been entirely ignored.

We agreed on a new strategy. The solicitors wrote to the airline informing them that unless the judgement debt was paid within the fixed period of time an application would be made to the Court to have me appointed Receiver of the assets of the airline.

I received a call from a very excited solicitor the following day to say that within hours of receiving their letter the airline had electronically transferred to the solicitors a sum of money well in excess of the judgement debt and the estimated legal costs, to head off the apparently distressing prospect of my future involvement as Receiver of their airline.

## Appointed Liquidator Behind Bars

Elsewhere in this book I talked about my unexpected encounter with a former inmate of Ford Open Prison, Gerald Ronson. It was for entirely unconnected reasons that I found myself visiting that establishment in 1989.

I had been consulted by the daughter of the chairman of a building company who, together with at least one other party, had been imprisoned at the end of a corruption trial arising out of the refurbishment of a famous London store's food hall. The imprisonment of the chairman left the company rudderless and its affairs in need of regularisation. The chairman was also the major shareholder and the most practical way of proceeding was to put the company into liquidation which would need a formal shareholders' meeting.

It being safe to assume that the Governor of the prison would not look favourably on a request that the chairman of the company be released from prison to pass a resolution for liquidation, I therefore sought and was granted permission to visit Mr X behind bars.

The formalities were carried out swiftly and without complication, but a few eyebrows were raised when the statutory notices in the national press recording my appointment as Liquidator in Ford Open Prison were spotted.

# Firm blames council after calling in receiver

A receiver has been called into wind up the construction firm of George Leatherbarrow Builders Limited, which was at the centre of a recent corruption trial. Yesterday an executive of the firm blamed part of the collapse on the local council, which he alleged has not paid a £200,000 bill.

On June 9, after an eight-week hearing at Liverpool Crown Court, George Leatherbarrow, Eric Spencer, the ex-chief architect of Kirkby, and council leader Dave Tempest were found guilty of conspiracy to corrupt.

The building firm was set up by the holding company, George Leatherbarrow Limited, to deal with Kirkby's Tower Hill estate, which involved the largest sums in the corruption trial.

Mr Leatherbarrow was sentenced to four years' imprisonment, Mr Stevenson to three years, and Mr Tempest to 12 months.

The prosecution said that the firm had received £10 millions worth of orders from the former Kirkby Council, on Merseyside, through bribes.

Mr David Powell, group company secretary, said yesterday the receiver had been called into the building firm but the two other companies in the group, Leatherbarrow Engineering and Leatherbarrow Plant Hire, had full order books and were making money.

Mr Powell said: "Creditors became afraid during the investigations and pressed for their money. Also, Kirkby Council still owe us £200,000."

Mr Powell added: "It was decided to cease trading as soon as our contracts were finished. That should be in about six months. We could have gone into liquidation 18 months ago, but we would have

taken a lot of people with us.

"Now we can devote more time to the other two companies which are making money," he said.

A spokesman for Knowsley Council, which has taken over from Kirkby Council, said: "They say we owe them money, but we maintain that they owe us money."

The spokesman added: "The Leatherbarrow group of companies were engaged on a number of projects for this council and in particular its predecessor, Kirkby Urban District Council. The council is still investigating these and, while it is sorry that one of the companies is going into receivership, it must be stated that in several matters the company has not yet presented financial accounts and in others there are substantial disputes over additional claims."

*Guardian* – 16th August 1978

## Corruption

In the previous tale I wrote about being appointed Liquidator by a director who had already been imprisoned.

In this next case, George Leatherbarrow Builders Ltd, I was appointed Receiver and Manager of an earth moving business where, not only a director of the company had been sent to prison, but also the local borough architect of a town well outside London. What had happened here was that, whilst on the face of it the earth moving company had been putting the earth it moved into an approved site, by collusion with various other parties it was, in fact, being used to build a slip road off an important new motorway leading into the city in question.

Even more bizarre, was the fact that the slip road was built in such a way that at most times of the day when motorists would be using it they would be driving straight into the sun, contrary to all logic and good practice. Unsurprisingly the architect was rapidly brought to book but took down the company with him.

To the best of my knowledge and belief the slip road remained in place but unused, a monument to the buccaneering 1980s!

## Sophie's Choice?

In the course of my career and certainly until the period of economic stability we've enjoyed for most of the last decade, the UK economy moved in a regular boom and bust cycle that became a cliché in the financial press. For insolvency practitioners, of course, business is counter-cyclical. In the early 1990s, in addition to everything else that was going on there was a massive property crash which threw up some big challenges.

At that time many European banks had wandered into the lending market in the United Kingdom having been seduced by the, apparently, guaranteed returns on lending to property developers.

I, and not a few other professional colleagues, were then kept very busy by those banks seeking to limit their losses.

The most unusual situation I encountered was when I was appointed Receiver of a development just behind Marylebone railway station in the West End of London. A very significant office block, which been financed by a Scandinavian bank, was half completed when the company developing it realised that it could not service its bank loans any further.

Having been appointed Receiver, detailed reviews were carried out to establish how much it would cost me to take personal liability to complete the development. Whilst this review was being carried out and in a melt-down property market environment, I was also exploring ways in which it might be possible to find buyers for the half completed development with a view to finishing it themselves.

The results of the first reviews of costs to complete came in at a frightening figure in the tens of millions of pounds. Much more disturbing was the deathly silence from the property development market from which I had expected some expressions of interest for buying and completing the project.

I could not simply sit there and wait indefinitely as the costs of maintenance, security and insurance were too significant.

I finally decided that I had to explore a third option which was one I had never explored before or since. I needed to compare the costs of the demolition of the half completed skyscraper with the likely current residual site value. These figures were obtained and for a while it looked as though, as paltry as the net yield would be from selling the site it was, if one took a pessimistic view of the medium term future of the property market, likely to be the least risky strategy.

After discussion with the lending bankers I was allowed to explore a strategy of letting it be known in the market place that I was seriously considering the demolition of the half completed development to, in a sense, call the bluff of those out there that might actually be privately taking a longer term and more benign view of the future of the property market. This proved to have been a good decision as very quickly interest started to be shown in acquiring the structure in Marylebone and a most satisfactory transaction, as far as the bank was concerned, was concluded.

Life After Debt

A lot of lenders in the early 1990s panicked, in what to them, was a foreign market place, and indeed a number of those secondary banks eventually found themselves in the hands of insolvency practitioners including me.

**False Economy** – *'It is false economy to go to bed early to save electricity if the result is twins!'*

Chinese Proverb

# Life After Debt

*Today* – 7th September 1992
Dave Gaskill

## Workers Co-operatives

In the 1960s, Tony Benn, the extraordinary and gifted politician, introduced the novel idea of Workers Co-operatives. A number were established, including Triumph Meriden, the motor cycle manufacturer and KME (Kirkby Manufacturing & Engineering) a central-heating radiator manufacturer in Liverpool.

Put at its simplest, the concept of a Workers Co-operative was that the workforce of a major failed business would receive finance to acquire the trading assets of that business as shareholders and hopefully run it profitably, with the profits going to the workers themselves.

For a variety of reasons, not least of which was a building slump, KME found itself in extremely deep water. Unusually, there was marked reluctance by the providers of its working capital, a clearing bank, to initiate insolvency proceedings, presumably out of anxiety about the potential political adverse publicity.

Whilst the creditors were dithering, the company's directors did exactly the right thing and consulted us as to what their own responsibilities and obligations were. We pointed out to them the risks of personal liability were they to be found to have carried on the business whilst they were aware of its insolvency and recommended in the absence of further sources of funding that liquidation be initiated.

The process of liquidation commences with a resolution of the company's shareholders. Our breath was taken away to have pointed out to us that each of the thousand workers in the factory, which occupied a mile long site on the outskirts of Liverpool, was a shareholder.

The logistics therefore of even commencing the liquidation presented a unique challenge.

After some discussion with the two representative directors a strategy was agreed and on a memorable day, Bernard and I and our team travelled to Kirkby at which a meeting of all the workforce had been convened to be addressed initially by their representative directors and then by Bernard.

Some of you may remember that the climate both politically and economically at that time was far from easy with attitudes hardening on both sides of the political spectrum. We were not at all sure how warmly our prospective involvement might be welcomed. I think it says a lot about the two indefatigable directors, as I recall Messrs Spriggs and Jenkins, and Bernard, that their respective addresses to the workforce persuaded them that it was in all parties best interests that they jointly resolved to place their company into liquidation. Inevitably it was a sombre factory that witnessed the sight of a thousand individuals queuing up to sign the requisite forms to place the company into immediate liquidation.

# The National Union Bank (NUB)

Another challenging client and a happy ending, just about!

In the 1950s and the 1960s a financial institution established its presence in the West End of London under the leadership of a Mr Teddy Smith. It went by the name of the National Union Bank which had its banking hall in Cavendish Square, London, W1. For reasons that never became clear to me I was telephoned one day by one of the bank's senior officers, a Mr ? to ask whether I would be prepared to act as Receiver and Manager of a substantial import/export business in north London. I looked at the figures and the security documentation and happily accepted the assignment which I could see was going to involve a lot of work, but was likely to be rewarding.

The assignment proceeded so well that the bank, within a very short period of time, had appointed me Receiver on three or four of their other defaulting loans. What this meant of course, was that at one particular point in time I was working almost exclusively on National Union Bank Receiverships.

After a couple of months my partners suggested that it was about time to talk about being paid something on account for the enormous amount of work that had been done, so I tried to broach the subject with the bank. In those early, heady days of Receiverships, fees were rather arbitrarily based, at a minimum, on the Law of Property Act, at 5% of the assets realised, which is what I thought was a prudent and conservative proposal to put to Mr ?. Sadly the client for either genuine or other reasons expressed great concern at our proposal and declined to make any payment until the assignments were completed.

# Life After Debt

The position for my firm was clearly untenable and we consulted lawyers about our problem with the client. We were, as we expected, advised that at the end of the day there was little doubt that fees that we would be awarded by a Court would be at least those we had conservatively sought, but what we needed was a pragmatic alternative to entering into litigation with the bank.

With a twinkle in his eye the partner in the firm of solicitors we had consulted suggested that as the proceeds of the assets of the cases that we had been handling were sitting in bank accounts in my name as Receiver at the National Union Bank, technically there was no reason why I could not simply draw a cheque for the total sums in the account and open an account in another bank. As attractive as that seemed, it did occur to us that any cheque drawn in that way might not be honoured by the bank, so with a double twinkle in his eye, the solicitor suggested that he and I walk to Cavendish Square, go to the banking hall and present a cash cheque to be drawn there and then over the counter.

Well that is what we set off to do that afternoon. We walked into the banking hall, presented a cash cheque for what was in those days at probably £200,000 – £250,000, an extremely significant sum of money and waited to see what happened. The look on the face of the cashier was nothing to compare with the look on the face of Mr ? when he appeared in the hall at the behest of the cashier and saw what was put into his hands.

He made it clear that he would not honour my cheque. I suspect that technically he should not have taken that decision but I had made my point.

As they say, there was a falling out, which resulted in my tendering my resignations on all the matters that I had been instructed on by the bank on condition I was paid my fees. The matter dragged on in litigation until ten minutes before the Court hearing was to take place, when literally on the steps of the Court my initial application for 5% was agreed by the bank, I was paid and I never worked for that bank again.

# German debt 'ruins firm'

DAVID MILLER got nothing but praise for the way his company organised most of the electronic scoreboard equipment at the 1972 Olympic Games in Munich.

He was congratulated by the then German Chancellor Willy Brandt.

But now the company, Associated Instrument Marketing has been forced into liquidation because, says Mr. Miller, the German authorities never paid up fully for the work.

The 22 employees have lost their jobs and at least £100,000 owed to the company's creditors. Mr. Miller, 49, said: "Ever since 1972 we have had a total of £85,000 tied up in Germany."

Mr. Miller started the company in 1967 with two other directors, Mr. Michael Houghton and Mr. Jack Farnfield,

**Sunday Express Reporter**

both 45. The company operated from Streatham Hill, London.

Its biggest boost came when it was awarded a £500,000 contract to produce scoreboard equipment for the Olympic Games.

Mr. Miller said: "We got 20 per cent of the money as a down payment and another 30 per cent on delivery of t h e equipment to Germany.

"The Olympic Building Group, the Government-backed company set up by the Germans to organise the building of the stadia and the Olympic village, seemed highly satisfied with the work.

"But trying to get the rest of the money became a real ordeal. Bits of it were paid over the next 18 months. "In the end we were still left with £45,000 owed to us by the Olympic Building Group and another £40,000 owed by the

German tax authorities in V.A.T. returns and refundable import tax.

The company's liquidator, accountant Mr. Peter Phillips, said: "It appears quite clear that the company has money quite legally owed to it by both the Olympic Building Group and the German tax authorities."

Dr. Dieter Hefter, business director of the Olympic Building Group, said: "They are not the victims of our organisation, only of themselves."

He confirmed that some money had been withheld, but added: "It was a much smaller sum than they say."

This has been done, he said, because after the games a s c o r e b o a r d had repeatedly failed to work properly.

Mr. Miller said later: "We have a telex message from Dr. Hefter saying all our equipment worked very satisfactorily."

# The Munich Olympics - 1972

This episode has nothing whatsoever to do with the appalling tragedy that occurred during the Munich Olympics when members of the Israeli Olympic team were taken hostage by the Palestinian organisation, Black September, and eleven of them were killed during an abortive rescue attempt by the German police.

My story suggests that there are a number of lessons of a much less grave nature to be learned from these four yearly events.

When London was more recently chosen as the next Olympic venue, the initial euphoria was gradually replaced by an awareness of the potential financial cost to the UK that will be inevitable. Over the last thirty or forty years there has been much speculation about the true benefits and burdens on cities that host Olympic Games and that certainly became clear to me when I found myself appointed Liquidator of a company known as Associated Instrument Marketing Ltd, a UK company that had designed and built the main electronic scoreboard for the Munich Olympics. The reason it eventually failed, after a very long period of negotiations with the Munich Olympic authorities was that it could not recover what it said was owed to it from those authorities.

What became apparent as I tried to press the claim, in those days approximately £400,000, was that economically the Olympic Games Authority in Munich had suffered terribly and that teams of individuals were now devoting themselves not to pursuing the Olympic dream but to minimising the outstanding liabilities of the Authority.

## Life After Debt

This story did not have a happy ending as, despite four or five years of my work and encouragement from the poor creditors, I eventually had to abandon the claim as creditors were not prepared to fund the inevitable litigation, and I simply could not work on into a sixth year having received no remuneration for the first five.

## A Horse, a Horse, my Kingdom...

Meetings of creditors are pretty significant events in the chronology of the demise of a company. Primarily, because they provide an open forum for the interrogation and criticism of all those associated with the failure, including the professionals delivering their report.

In the early 1970s we were consulted by representatives of a company known as Interkiln Ceramics Ltd. The company, which had been financed by the German State Funding Authorities, had built four brick making factories in North Africa. This business had found itself in enormous difficulties and its backers in Germany were not prepared to provide more funding, as they already faced loses to the tune of the tens of millions of pounds.

An attractive feature of the case was that amongst its assets was a large sum of money, in excess of £3 million, held in UK banks. From the potential Liquidator's point of view this offered the finest form of security for the large amount of work that was likely to have to be carried out on behalf of worldwide creditors.

There was, however, one particular hurdle to be overcome, if our firm was to remain in place as the shareholders' Nominee as Liquidators at the creditors' meeting. A lot of work went into preparing a detailed report on the circumstances that led to Interkiln's collapse and its Statement of Affairs (see Glossary). A large room was booked for the meeting of creditors in a London West End hotel and we arrived some time before the appointed time for the meeting with more than a few butterflies in our assembled stomachs. The butterflies became rather more active when the owners of the stomachs (us) realised that there were going to be some hundreds of creditors to report to at that meeting, all of whom would be entitled to ask some very pointed questions.

Bernard's presentation lasted well over an hour and I imagine any fatigue he might have been experiencing at the end of his presentation was obscured by a little bit of tension at how the next phase of the meeting, i.e. question time, was going to proceed.

He invited questions from the floor; there was a very long silence. From experience, very long silences at this stage of meetings of creditors were but a prelude to dramatic interventions by creditors or their representatives. Bernard allowed the silence to evolve. There was no intervention. My father presumably making allowances for the international nature of the audience that may not have fully understood that it was time for their enquiries to be dealt with, explained as clearly as he could what should then happen.

Still the silence... Could it be that no one was interested in why the company had collapsed?

This seemed to be unlikely so Bernard once again called for questions. Just as, he was about to cautiously proceed to the formal part of the meeting, namely the consideration of himself as Liquidator, a powerfully built man stood up in the centre of room and said in a strong middle-eastern accent, 'Mr Phillips I have a question'. I imagine it was not only just my own heart that sank at the prospect of this being the forerunner to many pointed questions. Bernard asked him to put his question and the man said, slowly and deliberately, 'I am only in London for two days, where can I buy a horse saddle?'

The words pin and drop came to mind, but Dad, ever the gentleman, responded by saying that, perhaps if the creditor would like to talk to him after the conclusion of the meeting he should be able to assist him.

That was the only question raised by creditors at the meeting, who proceeded then to happily and unanimously confirm Bernard as Liquidator and we got on with the very interesting job.

*Evening Standard* – February 1997
Paul Thomas

## Football, Football

In the 1990s a significant number of football clubs, and also rugby clubs, found themselves in financial difficulties. Not a few of those clubs fell to be dealt with by me and my partners.

Such beloved clubs as Luton Town, Millwall, Bradford City, Barnet, Oxford United, Leeds United, Tottenham Hotspur and Crystal Palace were helped by partners at Buchler Phillips and all clearly survived the experience.

The first professional encounter I had with a football club was when I was appointed Joint Liquidator in 1984 of Charlton Athletic. I believe that this was the first time that a football club went into formal liquidation.

This is an extremely short story, the main point of which is how I came to become involved. I was approached by a then senior director at Queens Park Rangers football club, which had found itself as a major, if not the biggest, creditor of Charlton Athletic. Charlton had not paid QPR for a celebrated footballer who had been transferred to them the previous season.

On the occasion of the Charlton Athletic meeting of creditors the vote of Queens Park Rangers resulted in my appointment as Joint Liquidator.

'No more training today lads,
the Receiver wants his ball'

*Daily Mail* – August 1982
Mahood

## Clients, even Banks, can be Embarrassing

Whilst for obvious reasons I will not be identifying the clearing bank involved in this story I know for a fact that they were no happier than I was after the event described in this short tale.

I and a partner were appointed Receivers and Managers of a very major company manufacturing houseware in the North of England. The enormous factory housed not merely stocks and the production line, but a vast shop-like environment where the company's wares were put on display.

The first few days of a case as complex as this always bring a multitude of tensions and challenges. An unexpected and unique one, occurred in this case.

In the middle of some tense negotiations with prospective purchaser for the business, I was telephoned from the display shop to be told that a senior officer of the clearing bank that had appointed me Receiver was there with his wife seeking to acquire without consideration some expensive items on display. Talk about an error of judgement on the part of the bank, but talk about embarrassment for me. I was left with no alternative of course but to confront the visitors and explain my view of proper and reasonable behaviour.

The good news is that the visitors left, in due course the business was sold and my relationship with the bank survived.

# Life After Debt

# The Fourth Estate

*'News is to journalism what dung is to rhubarb.'*

Ian Jack, *Sunday Times'* journalist

## The Fourth Estate

It has become as fashionable, acceptable and easy to bad mouth the media as it is to attack politicians.  It has certainly seemed to my profession that it has been cared for by the Press in no less combative a manner.

Maybe surprisingly, my own perspective is that until the Maxwell fees issue was presented to the media I had much more to thank them for than to grouse about over a pretty long career.  The work that I and my colleagues found ourselves doing often involved household names and/or challenging human issues.  I think it is fair to say that provided one dealt professionally and clearly with the media there was not only little to fear but very often considerable benefit in giving the public a window into one's strategy at the time for this case or the other.

Maybe the best example is that when I was appointed Maxwell's Receiver no one knew where his last will and testament were and therefore I issued a press release appealing to anybody who might know its whereabouts to let me know.  The following day a very well known firm of international lawyers telephoned me to say they were delivering to me, by hand, a copy of the document I needed.  On other occasions the publicity given to the collapse of a company and its implicit availability for acquisition brought potential buyers to my door.

In mid-career I used to meet cub reporters on professional magazines like *Accountancy Age* who found themselves having to look for stories in the insolvency arena.  I seemed to have many such stories and spent a fair time with these cub reporters who eventually moved on to the national dailies, the heavyweights and even to starting their own publications.

# Oz

I do hope that a number of you who are reading this book do not need reminding about the extraordinary time in post-war British history when Hippiedom and Flower Power convinced not a few that all the world's problems had been resolved and that together we could look forward to eternal happiness.

As distinct from the political realities or unrealities of all of that, I found myself involved with the care of some of the financial casualties of those stimulating times.

The most interesting for me, was being consulted by Richard Neville, Jim Anderson and Felix Dennis, the directors of Oz Publications. A household name in the early 1970s, the magazine Oz pushed the limits of public tolerance with sexually explicit anti-establishment material.

In the notorious School Kids issue, material about a certain school master caused him such offence that he commenced a libel action against the magazine. Its three directors were charged under the Obscene Publications Act and tried at the Old Bailey in 1971.

Oz was one of several underground publications targeted by the Obscene Publications Squad. Directors Neville, Dennis and Anderson were charged with 'conspiracy to corrupt public morals' which in theory carried a virtually unlimited penalty. Their defence lawyer, John Mortimer QC, announced at the opening of the trial in 1971, that 'the case stands at the crossroads of our liberty, at the boundaries of our freedom to think and draw and write what we please' (The Times 24 June 1971).

# Life After Debt

John Lennon and Yoko Ono joined the protest march against the prosecution and organised a recording of 'God Save Oz' to raise funds and gain publicity.

The trial was, at the time, the longest obscenity trial in British legal history.  Defence witnesses included comedian Marty Feldman, John Peel, musician and writer George Melly and academic, Edward De Bono.

At the conclusion of the trial the 'Oz Three' were found guilty and sentenced to hard labour, although Felix Dennis was given a lesser sentence as the judge, Mr Justice Michael Argyle, considered that Dennis was *very much less intelligent* than Neville and Anderson.

In this particular context it is illuminating to bear in mind that Felix Dennis over the last few years has regularly appeared in *The Sunday Times* 1000 Rich List as a result of a highly successful career in publishing.

Shortly after the verdicts were handed down the three directors were taken to prison and their heads shaved.

The most famous images of the trial come from the committal hearing at which Neville, Dennis and Anderson all appeared wearing rented schoolgirl costumes!

At the appeal hearing, where the defendants appeared wearing long wigs, it was found that Mr Justice Argyle has grossly misdirected the jury on numerous occasions.  Their convictions were overturned.

# OZ

LAST TEN
COPIES

## SCHOOL KIDS ISSUE

Offers to The Liquidator - Oz Publications INK Limited
PETER PHILLIPS, 7b New Cavendish Street, London W1M 8AH.
Tel: 01 580 0784

**IMPORTANT NOTICE**
As a result of the police prosecution these copies of OZ
may not be sent through the post.

## OZ 47

FINAL ISSUE BEFORE LIQUIDATION
LAST TEN THOUSAND COPIES
Offers to The Liquidator - OZ Publications INK Limited
PETER PHILLIPS, 76 New Cavendish Street, London W1M 8AH
Tel. 01 580 0784

## NASTY TALES NO.1

Released by Police after unsuccessful prosecution
LAST 150 COPIES
75p each including P&P or offers for the lot to the Liquidator,
Bloom Publications Limited PETER PHILLIPS, 76 New Cavendish
Street, London W1M 8 AH. Tel: 01 580 0784

*Daily Mail* – 23rd August 1973

*Private Eye*
24th August, 1973

## Oz acquires a curious respectability

There is a delicate irony in the task of accountant Mr Peter Phillips, whose time is presently devoted to getting money for the creditors of two publishing companies who produced underground newspapers.

He sits in his West End office in New Cavendish Street waiting for replies to an advertisement offering for sale copies of *Oz* and *Nasty Tales* —publications that deeply disturbed middle class mores.

As liquidator for the two companies — a sturdy Establishment role — the 28-year-old Mr Phillips, a partner of the chartered accountants Bernard Phillips and Co.—he views his job with an element of philosophical resign.

Mr Phillips has for sale the last 10 copies of the *Oz School-kids Issue*

He also has 10,000 copies of *Oz 47* for sale, the final issue

And then he has 150 copies of *Nasty Tales Number 1*, the underground comic

Debts outstanding: *Oz* owes £21,000 to creditors and Bloom £9,000.

# Life After Debt

Running along parallel lines, legally speaking, was a civil action by the schoolmaster who was awarded damages the size of which drove the magazine into liquidation. Creditors were unlikely to receive any dividend as the remaining assets were so small, but I was handed by the directors the last eight or so unsold copies of the offending issue.

I was urged to offer them for sale as collectors' items, but it was pointed out to me by lawyers that I would be unable to sell them without exposing myself to the charge of publishing a libel, the very thing that had brought the company down.

I contacted the libelled party and obtained his permission to offer the magazines for sale in the hope that it would produce some dividend against his claim. The proviso was that I attached to any magazine sold a copy of the libel judgement.

Thinking I was now free to sell the magazines, I was disappointed to then discover that I would be unable to send them through the post to any successful purchaser, as that would contravene the Obscene Publications Act, and thereby be exposed to criminal charges!

I eventually advertised the remaining copies in *Private Eye*, pointing out that any successful purchaser would have to call personally at my offices to pay for and collect their acquisition. This is exactly what happened and some thousands of pounds were realised this way.

I have often wondered whether the former directors of the magazine got some pleasure and saw not a little irony in the final turn of events.

## Time Out

Time Out is another celebrated name in publishing.

Its best known product is the *Time Out* weekly listings magazine. The original magazine with listings for London was published in 1968 by Tony Elliot, who remains the owner of the group, which in 2003 reported revenues of £25 million.

2004 data indicates that fifteen cities around the world were serviced by the group, including Chicago, New York, Paris, Mexico City, Beijing, Dubai, Istanbul, Tel Aviv, Cyprus, Moscow, Athens and Beirut.

What it is probably less well known is that in 1970 Tony Elliot set up Time Out in Manchester Ltd. and that it was not a success. I can say that because he appointed me as its Liquidator.

It seems to me that this is just one of a large number of examples I could quote of our most successful entrepreneurs encountering minor, in this case, but in many cases, quite major blips on their road to triumph.

## Gay News

*Gay News*, a fortnightly newspaper published in the UK, was founded in 1972 in collaboration between the Gay Liberation Front and the Campaign for Homosexual Equality.

The Editor, Dennis Lemmon, was charged and fined for obstruction, and for taking photographs of police behaviour outside a popular Earls Court leather bar, The Coleherne.

In 1974 *Gay News* was charged with obscenity, having published a cover photograph of two men kissing. It won the court case. In 1976 and 1977 Mary Whitehouse brought a prosecution against both the magazine and its editor for the publication of poem 'The Love that Dares to Speak Its Name'.

Lemmon was found guilty and sentenced to a suspended eighteen-month prison sentence, with fines and costs awarded against him and *Gay News* amounting to nearly £10,000.

After a campaign and an appeal to remove his prison sentence was dropped, one of the biggest problems the magazine faced was that although not an obscene publication it found it very hard to find sales outlets. WHSmith refused to sell it and to allow their distribution company to distribute it to other suppliers. Various campaigns were organised by the gay community to shame WH Smith into allowing the magazine to be sold by them, with a successful outcome.

Its travails brought it to the doors of our offices and they asked Percy Phillips, my uncle, and founder of the firm in which I and Bernard worked, to handle the liquidation.

## Life After Debt

Creditors appointed Percy as Liquidator and as a token of the directors' gratitude for his sensitive handling of all the issues they presented him with a letter rack with large kitsch gold lettering on the front of it spelling out the incantation *Do it now*!

The younger members of the office inevitably found it quite hysterical to see on the desk of a very staid septuagenarian accountant, Percy Phillips, a tribute of this nature.

## A Good Press

insolvency practitioners have learned over the years that whatever else they want in terms of career satisfaction they should not expect to be treated well by the press.

In the early years of the media's awareness of liquidations and Receiverships, curiosity and maybe even admiration coloured their reporting of my professions' activities.  That soon became replaced by an obsession with the perceived parasitical nature of our work and, the perceived extortionate nature of what we were paid to do it.

Perhaps the most charming exception to this was when I was appointed Receiver of what was variously known as the *West Wales Weekly Observer* and the *Tenby Gazette*.  This was a long established and much loved regional journal with a staff of only a dozen industrious and loyal individuals.

The company that owned the journal had run out of working capital and as Receiver I could see that, whilst I could operate the newspaper on a hand-to-mouth basis for maybe two or three weeks, unless a purchaser was found for it, it would have to close very quickly.

Unsurprisingly, the reportage of my receivership and the explanation of its objectives was sympathetic, accurate and encouraging.  This reportage however, was only available in the *Tenby Gazette*!

Life After Debt

The happy ending to this story is that, Ray Tindle, a well known newspaper proprietor, took a personal interest in this journal and bought it from me as Receiver to keep it alive.

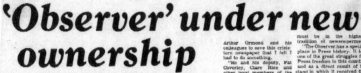

# 'Observer' under new ownership

After months of struggle and uncertainty, the 'Weekly Observer', one of Wales' oldest newspapers, has been saved from extinction. The paper has been published this week under the helm of new owners.

On Monday afternoon contracts were exchanged in London following a week of intense negotiation.

Principal figure in the takeover has been one of the best-known and respected men in provincial newspapers, Mr. Ray Tindle, O.B.E., Chairman and managing director of Farnham Castle Newspapers Ltd., of Farnham, Surrey.

Mr. Tindle finally clinched the deal by telephone while visiting Tenby with his general manager, Mr. Dennis Stone.

A new company, Regent Weekly Newspapers Ltd., based in the paper's existing offices in South Parade, Tenby, has been formed.

The "Weekly Observer" will revert to its former titles of 'Tenby Observer' and 'Weekly News' (Narberth and Whitland edition) and will continue to be published and printed in the Tenby works by the same staff. At least a dozen jobs have been saved by the rescue bid.

Mr. Tindle who was President of the Newspaper Society in 1971-72, and is currently Chairman of its Press Freedom Committee, is also Chairman of Surrey Advertiser Ltd., Aldershot News Ltd., London and Westminster Newspapers Ltd., and City of London Recorder Ltd. He was awarded the O.B.E. in 1973 for services to the news

And despite many problems, including a very tight time factor, he succeeded.

When he read a fortnight ago of the financial threat to the future of the 'Tenby Observer' he determined to make every effort to save it.

In a statement issued immediately after the purchase had been finalised, Mr. Tindle said:

"I was so impressed by the prolonged struggle of Editor Arthur Ormond and his colleagues to save this crisis-torn newspaper that I felt I had to do something.

"He and his deputy, Pat Coveley, Clare Rice and other loyal members of the staff, have kept this 125-year-old paper going for months in the face of the severest financial and production difficulties that can be imagined. On many weeks there has not even been the certainty of wage packets.

"This loyalty to the paper must be in the highest tradition of newspapermen.

"The Observer has a special place in Press history. It led one of the great struggles for Press freedom in this country and as a direct result of its stand in which it received the support of Lord Northcliffe and other leading newspapermen of the day - all newspapers gained the right to attend and report meetings of Councils.

"The Tenby Observer's battle resulted in the passing of the Admission of the Press Act 1908. Seventy years later this famous newspaper is engaged in another fight - this time for its life.

"My colleague Dennis Stone and I will do everything we can to help this plucky staff to win through.

"I should like to place on record the assistance of John Harrison, Kenneth Loughnan and Gough Devereux and our deep appreciation of our readers and advertisers whose continued support we now earnestly seek as we set about the task of putting the paper back on a sound commercial footing".

PHOTO: MALCOLM RICHARDS

Thumbs up from the staff after Monday's announcement. On the right Editor Arthur Ormond and Deputy Editor Pat Coveley.

*Tenby Gazette*

*The Sunday Times* – 15th August 1982
Calman

## The Best Laid Plans...

In the very early 1980s the marketing department of the *Financial Times* took an initiative which survives to this day. It offered insolvency practitioners a regular part of the Tuesday and Friday editions in which to advertise their wares i.e. companies over which they had been appointed Receiver, Liquidators or Administrators (see glossary) where they were hoping to attract interest from buyers on a going-concern basis. During times of recession many such adverts would appear each week, and some people took as a barometer of a changed economic climate the paucity of such adverts at other times.

This was a unique concept by the *Financial Times* and the clearest tribute to it was that it ultimately became an almost indispensable part of the insolvency practitioners' tool kit when disposing of any business. To explain, if there was, and there often was, criticism of insolvency practitioners for allegedly not marketing as widely as possible what they have to sell, showing that one had advertised in the FT became regarded as almost notice to the world.

On one excruciating occasion however, the system backfired. By the system, I mean, the practice that understandably evolved, of firms like mine at the time, Arthur Andersen, in informed anticipation of being appointed Receiver etc of a business, placing, provisionally, advertisements in the forthcoming Business for Sale page in the FT. These were placed with clear instructions that they could be withdrawn on demand and as late as the day before publication. This was obviously a necessary precaution to avoid the advertising of failed businesses that had not failed.

You have probably already sensed where this story is going and you are probably right.

On the one occasion that both the FT and my then firm would prefer to forget, an advertisement had been placed provisionally with the FT, and on the day before its planned publication it was withdrawn, as a decision was taken by the company and its bankers that Receivership was not at that stage the best option.

The next morning, incandescent calls were received from the Board of the subject company after they had been telephoned by all sorts of people commiserating with them on their Receivership as announced in the FT that morning.

The best one can say about all of this is that there had been a communication breakdown.  It never happened again to the best of my knowledge.  Somehow civil relations survived between all the parties involved.

## A Visit to the Chancellor's

Just as there is life after debt I experienced life before debt. Like most excitable students I sought unconventional ways of communicating messages about my view of the establishment.

I was afforded a wonderful opportunity by a good friend of mine at the time. His fiancée was a best friend of Carolyn Maudling, the daughter of the then Chancellor of the Exchequer, Reginald Maudling.  We had all been invited to a Saturday night party at, yes, No 11 Downing Street.  It is difficult to believe that in the early 1960s the political climate in terms of Home Security was so much gentler, that I, together with others going to the party on a Saturday night, could actually park our cars in Downing Street without fear of anything, even parking wardens.  I knocked on the door, was let in by the statutory officer and had a very nice evening indeed.

Some juvenile part of me had decided, some days before, that I really wanted to leave a message for Government and so I had taken in to No 11, in the inside pocket of a jacket I was wearing, that day's edition of the *Daily Worker* (now the *Morning Star*) and took enormous pride in leaving it propped up above the toilet of that fine establishment.

# Insolvency Colleagues and Standards

*'It's an Insolvency Practitioner'*

*The Times* – 21st March 1991
Ken Pyne

## Insolvency Colleagues and Standards

There is no question in my mind that throughout the forty years of my career an absolutely key element in the pleasure it gave me was the extraordinary, and I suspect unique, nature of the relatively small group of people calling themselves insolvency practitioners. This group of maybe 150 people, who around the United Kingdom were seen as 'the key players', were not simply, like me, accountants or lawyers. Some were specialist bankers, business valuation experts and representatives of trade associations.

Whilst, of course, fundamentally, many of us were each other's direct competitors, nevertheless there was an extraordinary camaraderie amongst these players and their teams which was reinforced by the conferences and social events organised primarily by the Insolvency Practitioners Association from the early 1960s.

I trust this explains why a number of stories in this book are about some of those friends and all of them have been written with affection and respect.

*The Times* - 20th November 1980
Marc Boxer

## Maybe I should have been a Doctor?

At about the age of ten it was becoming pretty obvious to me how bad my handwriting was.  This awareness was shared by my teachers, one of whom was extremely kind and told me that in her experience people of my then age with appalling handwriting turned into adults with excellent handwriting.
I regret to say that she was wrong.

Whilst one of the lesser inconveniences of my disability includes my bank occasionally having to reject cheques I have issued because of an inconsistency of signature, early in my career I suffered a much more severe embarrassment.

The first task I was given when I started working for my father was to write out about a thousand cheques to creditors of a liquidated company who were to receive their first dividend.
I remember the name of the case very well.  It was Oliver Industries and Bernard was joint Liquidator of the company with a Mr J. Ness Prentiss of one of the most eminent accounting firms, then Deloitte Plender Griffiths.

It was with no pride but with considerable relief that after several days, I despatched the completed cheques to Mr Prentiss for his signature before placing them before Bernard. Later that week I was called to my father's office, handed the cheque books and invited to read the letter that accompanied them.

In short (in very short) Mr Prentiss was returning the cheques to be re-drawn as, in his view, the writing on most of them was entirely illegible.  Dad, as ever, let me down extremely lightly.

## Life After Debt

He could see that sufficient chastisement was going to be heaped by me on myself the minute I escaped his room.

# Fire Officer Mr Leonard Curtis

Leonard Curtis was for many years a very well known insolvency practitioner in London, whose firm specialised in dealing with the affairs of companies and individuals falling on hard times in the clothing industry.

Leonard was an extraordinary character with a wicked sense of humour. He was also as they say, not one with whom one should lightly cross swords.

Like many other successful practitioners, he was trained by Bernard and Percy. He commenced his apprenticeship with them during the Second World War when they occupied offices in Langham Place, London, just opposite BBC Broadcasting House.

One night Bernard and Percy were telephoned by the London Fire Brigade to say that a bomb that hit the BBC building had devastated the Phillips' own offices and that they should come up to the bomb site without delay.

They arrived at about the same time; Percy being extremely concerned that that very afternoon he had taken over the bankruptcy of an Indian begum and taken possession of a significant amount of valuable jewellery which he had placed in the office safe overnight. He instructed the firemen wading through all that was left of the office premises to dig for the safe.

# Life After Debt

Bernard had a different concern and that was for Leonard Curtis who had been on fire duty that evening. He encouraged the firemen to dig for Leonard.

After an hour or two there was a yell from a group of firemen who had found the safe. Percy put his key in its lock and the door opened without difficulty. He took possession of the jewellery for the night and put it in a safe deposit the next morning.

It was sometime after that, as Bernard was anxiously watching the firemen search for Leonard, when he was tapped on the shoulder and turned around to see Leonard looking at him and apparently uninjured.

My father enquired, 'Are you alright?' and Leonard said, 'Yes, I'm fine. I've been down at the pub, what's happened?'

I suspect that maybe a generation of both creditors and directors have that night to thank, for the unique career that Leonard Curtis went on to enjoy.

## Location, Location

76, New Cavendish Street, the address of Bernard Phillips and Co, was an extraordinary place for the Phillips family to have spent over thirty years. Amongst the many bizarre experiences were the intermittent arrivals of individuals looking to talk to someone about their problems but asking for people who didn't work at the firm. It became clear that these visitors were in fact destined for number 76a New Cavendish Street, the then premises of the Marriage Guidance Council. Added poignancy was provided by the intermittent misdelivery of large quantities of boxes of Kleenex tissues.

They say what goes around comes around and one of the ways I am spending my time post-retirement from accountancy, is counselling couples on behalf of Relate which in the days of New Cavendish Street was the Marriage Guidance Council.

## Just in Case you get Ahead of Yourself

The Bernard Phillips and Leonard Curtis practices were geographically close in the West End of London, in the heart of 'Doctor Land', and we often found ourselves working together on joint assignments.

The day arrived when my father's new young partner, me, and Leonard's new young partner, a Mr Phillip Monjack, were allowed to act jointly for the first time. The case itself was not complicated, large or particularly interesting, but the most entertaining feature of the entire assignment was when Phillip Monjack and I were invited to sign the various statutory documents confirming our appointment in Leonard Curtis's office, shortly after the meetings of shareholders and creditors.

Leonard sat us both down in front of him and asked his PA to bring in the documents for our signature. They were placed before me, and just as I was about to put pen to paper, scanning the first documents I saw, just as I heard a cackle of laughter come from Leonard, the recitation 'the shareholders resolved that Master Ian Peter Phillips and that Master Phillip Monjack be appointed Joint Liquidators'.

Well, time passes and did pass and in due course Phillip Monjack became senior partner of Leonard Curtis & Co and I became chairman of the firm that in many respects was the successor to my father's practice, Buchler Phillips & Co.

# Christopher Morris

Most chapters in this book are devoted to household names in the sense of companies and individuals whose financial challenges have involved me and my partners.

This one is about another insolvency practitioner who became a household name, and celebrated by the creditors of Laker Airways. He, as that airline's Liquidator, successfully sued British Airways and other airlines. He eventually settled out of court enabling Laker Airways to pay off its debts.

Chris Morris's career, like my own, started off very much more modestly. In fact, he joined my firm shortly after I qualified as a chartered accountant. For the better part of two years we shared a room and a number of exciting professional and culinary experiences, until he decided to move out of insolvency and back into auditing, a decision which was short-lived, as within a year he had joined, what was then, Touche Ross, where he eventually became Head of their Insolvency Division.

The point of this particular tale is not so much to show how generous I can be to other professionals (and competitors) but to recall the day on which I presided over my first ever meeting of creditors. The name of the company will forever remain etched on my memory, High Fidelity Musical Products Ltd.

Chairing meetings of creditors has always been an unpredictable and stressful task; therefore Bernard had allocated me a company with virtually no creditors and no other issues to confront for my *launch*.

# Life After Debt

I nevertheless, spent a number of sleepless nights preparing for the meeting, taking no consolation from my colleagues who told me there was nothing to worry about.

The meeting was arranged for 2.30 pm and I had no appetite, leaving Chris to go off for lunch to our favourite kebab house on his own.

He returned just before 2 o'clock and rushed into our room looking, for the only time that I can recall, seriously flustered.

I asked him what the matter was and he told me that there was an enormous group of people assembling downstairs for the meeting of creditors for a company that as I said earlier, we had been told by the director had few creditors.

That group had heard him welcomed back by our receptionist as Mr Morris and had set about him mistaking him for the Mr Morris who was the Chairman and Director of High Fidelity Musical Products Ltd!

What transpired during the afternoon was that the other Mr Morris had forgotten to tell us that there were 120 members of the public who had paid £1000 each for goods they had not received – that they had somehow found out when and where a meeting of creditors was taking place and quite properly decided to come along to vent their spleen.

I think it is safe to say that I had an even more uncomfortable afternoon than Chris Morris had a lunch hour. Maybe because of, rather than despite that awful day, we have remained excellent friends ever since.

## The Three-Day Week and a Mr John Talbot

This is, if you like, a tale with two morals: one is how every cloud has a silver lining and two, how stars can be found in the most unlikely places.

Darocain Ltd was a tie manufacturing business in Corby, Northamptonshire.  In the early 1970s the company's bankers appointed Bernard Receiver and Manager, and he and I took over a large factory with a big workforce making what seemed to be nothing but very colourful Kipper ties.  The business had lost a fortune and unless a buyer could be found for the trading assets there would be hundreds of people laid off.

Our team worked extremely hard and was assisted in its endeavours by a young man who had recently been appointed Darocain's Company Secretary, a chartered accountant with an unusual amount of talent.  Thanks to our ability to hold the business together whilst it was offered for sale, a large public company from Nottingham agreed to purchase the business.

On the day the transaction was scheduled to be completed, Bernard took the train to Nottingham and spent the day completing the documentation, obtaining the appropriate consents from local authorities etc, signing on the many dotted lines and banking the purchaser's Bankers Drafts before 3.00 pm – then bank closing time.

My father made his way back to the railway station and picked up a copy of the evening paper (a choice then, of three!) to read its banner headlines 'Three Day Week' in block letters.  What this heralded was that the Government, under the late

Life After Debt

Edward Heath, which had been struggling to contain the unrest caused by the miners' strike, and the resultant fuel shortages, had taken an historic step in imposing severe constraints on the use of energy throughout the United Kingdom.

What was good for the creditors of Darocain was the exact opposite for the unfortunate purchaser who, if it had transacted a few hours later, would certainly not have bought the business.

Within six weeks the business that had just been sold was closed down again, this time for keeps.

The other, entirely unexpected, yield from this assignment was the company secretary. Whilst the purchaser of the business took the entire workforce of the business with him, he did not need the company secretary and laid him off. I had a very strong sense that this young man would do very well in my profession and I persuaded him to come and work with me, which he did for two years, commuting daily from Leicester.

This young man was John Talbot, an individual, who in the course of his career, which is still running, has become generally regarded as an icon in the business reorganisation and restructuring profession.

He is probably bored stiff with being reminded of his appearance when I first met him. He had shoulder length hair, flared trousers and the statutory Kipper tie!

He took over as head of Arthur Andersen's Insolvency group from me in 1986 and joined Kroll a few months before I retired from that firm in 2005.

## Value of a Professional Qualification!

For most of my professional life I was in partnership with David Buchler, a young man who became my articled clerk in the same year that I married my wife, Wendy, 1970. David, like many in the insolvency profession is a one off, with some extraordinary talents. He has known me too long to mind my suggesting that, on occasion, diplomacy has not always been his best suit.

This little story, which has not been embellished at all, arose from one of the regular lecturing trips David and I used to make to Hong Kong. These seemed to coincide with the Hong Kong Rugby 7s and we used to combine the rigours of practice development with the challenges of sporting pursuits and dining well.

David, at the time, was between marriages and on the evening in question, David, his companion at the time, Tessa, and I were returning to the Grand Hyatt Hotel, exhausted by all of the challenges referred to earlier, late in the evening.

We just had enough energy to slump in the Champagne Bar at the Grand Hyatt whilst David said he needed to go to Reception to confirm some quite complex travel arrangements starting the following morning.

Tessa and I were happily waiting for our refreshments when an uncharacteristically David anxiously rushed in to the bar, sat down next to us and said, 'They're after me'.

# Life After Debt

I tried unsuccessfully to obtain a better understanding of what he was talking about until he looked up and pointed at the door to the bar and said, 'There they are'.

Tessa and I followed the direction of David's finger and saw strolling menacingly through the door six slim young men in what appeared to be black combat outfits.

They looked around the bar, then pointed at David, shouted, 'That's him!' and rushed over. They literally picked David up and started running out of the bar with him.

Whatever may or may not have been my achievements or lifelong qualities, martial arts and physical courage have not been generally regarded as the most obvious.

Nevertheless, and presumably because of the robust condition I had been left by the evening's indulgences, I jumped up, strode over to the struggling group leaving the bar and shouted 'Stop!'

Although I was a little surprised when my order was obeyed, I pressed on by saying, 'Put him down, he's my partner'. The group of six abductors looked at me very strangely and in a way that in normal circumstances would have had me running in the opposite direction whilst checking my life policies.

On this unique occasion however I had a final trump up my sleeve, or so it turned out. I shouted at them, 'He is a Chartered Accountant'. Lord knows where that came from, but the impact it had has never left me. The group dropped David to the floor and he absented himself with his usual fine body-eye co-ordination.

# Life After Debt

Meanwhile, Tessa had come up behind me and took over. She shouted at the group of six abductors, 'It's not him' pointing to the departing David, 'It's him' at someone I couldn't even see on the far side of the vast lush Grand Hyatt bar.

The final part of this crazy sequence was that the group of six then tore over to the other side of the bar; picked up the stranger Tessa had pointed out and ran away with him!

I caught up with David a few minutes later and demanded an explanation for what was going on. Apparently, when David had gone to clarify his ticket reservation for the following morning, what he was told suggested to him that there had been an enormous mess up which looked incapable of resolution.

David regrettably had lost his cool and had so upset the receptionist that security was called and that security took the form of the platoon that was sent in after him to the bar where I was hoping to enjoy a peaceful night cap.

*'Pushy is someone that goes through a set of swing doors behind and comes out ahead!'*

## Polly Peck

Polly Peck is a story of a missed assignment and a missed gourmet lunch.

Many of you should recall the economic climate in 1990. It was rather like 2010 and dire. It was the year in which many large corporations failed. One of which, British & Commonwealth, I have discussed earlier.

One major international bank were so pleased with David Buchler and I for work that we had been doing for them that they invited us up to their City head office, to a dining room on the top floor with, as I recall it, a domed ceiling where their two top risk directors proposed to entertain us in style with a private luncheon.

1990 was the year in which both David and I girded our loins with mobile telephones, business tools which had just come onto the market. As totally unsophisticated users of these devices we had not thought to switch them off and just as I was enjoying my first pre-luncheon cocktail the bell rang on my belt. I felt extremely embarrassed and proposed to ignore the call, but our amused hosts insisted I answered it.

When I did, I found that I was talking to the senior partner of one of the Big Four accounting practices, Michael Jordan of Coopers & Lybrand, who informed me that an application was being made to the Court in the near future for Administrators to be appointed to Polly Peck.

# Life After Debt

Polly Peck was a company that had been the subject of continuing Press interest from the time that it was acquired by a Mr Asil Nadir from the family owners of the business who for decades had run a successful garment manufacturing business.

Polly Peck's business, under Mr Nadir, had then developed in all sorts of ways, most apparently in orange juice production in northern Cyprus.

The share price had done extraordinary things, leaping to ever new heights, until the wheels started falling off the company, and in particular, off Mr Nadir's credibility.

Returning to my position at the time, waiting for lunch with some important hosts in the City, I ask my caller Michael Jordan whether I could ring him back and was told that the subject he wished to discuss with me was urgent.

I left my hosts and went to another room, where, it became clear that what I was being asked was whether I would be prepared to act as one of the Administrators of Polly Peck to handle such aspects of the work where otherwise Coopers & Lybrand might be regarded as having a conflict.

This concept was not novel and in fact was the basis on which I acted as one of the Administrators of British & Commonwealth, alongside partners in Ernst & Young.

There were all sorts of professional and other issues whirring through my mind as in need of careful deliberation before I could give my consent, I sought to explain this to Mr Jordan, another extraordinarily successful and highly regarded insolvency practitioner, but who was also known for not beating around the bush.

He explained in very few words that as the application was being heard in 30 minutes time the best use of my next 30 minutes would be to catch a taxi to the Royal Courts of Justice.

As they have said in more widely distributed tomes than this, it was really an offer I couldn't refuse. I returned to my hosts and preserving suitable confidentiality explained my dilemma.

I put myself on their mercy and asked to be excused from the luncheon. The hosts were perfect gentlemen, thoroughly amused by developments, and in wishing me good fortune pointed out that what I was now going to be missing was sharing with David and the two of them a lunch personally prepared by Michel Roux who was in their kitchens that day!

I reached Court in time and with a rumbling stomach, sat through an afternoon of complex applications and cross-applications by various interested parties. The result of all this was that I did not become one of the Administrators of Polly Peck, but in fact my old friend, Chris Morris, of the Touche Ross (see Christopher Morris) worked alongside Michael Jordan as Joint Administrator.

From what I have learned of the challenges that everyone associated with the Polly Peck administration had to face, including the murder of one of the accounting firms managers in Turkey, I am in no doubt that whilst I certainly missed out on an excellent lunch someone was taking good care of me in keeping me away from Polly Peck.

*The Guardian* - 8th January 1991
Austin

## The Start of a Wonderful Friendship

Right at the beginning of the 1980s one of my first challenges as a newly appointed partner in Arthur Andersen was to travel to New York and make a presentation to the leading lawyers and bankers in that city about the new area of practice I was heading for that firm.

Arthur Andersen was, as ever, at the leading edge of technology in client service and suggested I used a PowerPoint presentation.

This suggestion filled me with apprehension for a number of reasons, not least which was that at that time I had never touched a computer in my life. Neither had I ever made a PowerPoint presentation.

I was put into the care of the Andersen department that existed at that time to design computer presentations. They assured me that everything would be done for me and then all that I would have to do on the day would be to press a button on a keyboard.

Enormous care was taken to ensure that the presentation was downloaded onto disks of which three copies were made. One was sent surface mail in silver foil to the New York office, one similarly wrapped and carried in my luggage and the third in my carry-on luggage. I dutifully arrived at New York and was given two or three hours to practice my presentation in the Arthur Andersen training suites on 6th Avenue.

# Life After Debt

The training suites and presentation rooms were extraordinary in that they appeared to be carpeted not merely wall to wall but wall to ceiling. The significance of that became apparent when I started my presentation.

The presentation room was full to overflowing with about 200 of the great and the good in banking and law and I was introduced generously by the New York managing partner who winked at me encouragingly as I strode to the podium.

Following weeks of preparation I pressed a key on the computer. There was a loud crack and a flash of light as the static electricity that I had accumulated in my body during the afternoon found a way out!

The PowerPoint presentation and the computer simultaneously crashed, leaving me in need of support, when like a voice from on high, came the immortal words, 'Reboot it Pete'.

I had to pause as I did not know what 'reboot' might have meant and I certainly didn't think that anyone in the room knew me well enough to call me Pete.

I invited the anonymous advisor to step forward. A man strode from the back of the room up to my computer, fiddled with it for a couple of minutes and got it working. I shook his hand, he returned to the back of the room and I completed what turned out to be a very successful presentation. Needless to say when it was all over I dashed over to re-acquaint myself with my saviour, who turned out to be a Mr Adrian Mariette, an extremely senior official, of the then, Midland Bank. I owed that man more than a dinner, but over a dinner is how I started to get to know one of the more engaging characters in my professional career. Adrian eventually came to work in London for both the Midland Bank and HSBC and over many years we found ourselves involved in all sorts of stimulating assignments, some of the more important of which even involved us being on opposing sides.

## You can't be all Things to all People

I consider the fact that my parents were from different religious backgrounds a blessing.  My father came from an orthodox Jewish upbringing to atheism and my mother remained throughout her life a very privately spiritual person after a Wesleyan type upbringing.  She introduced me to the delights of carol singing and so some years ago, in the lead up to Christmas, and perhaps unwisely in the north-west London suburb in which we have always lived, Wendy and I joined a group of carol singers going from door-to-door.

We were having a thoroughly good evening when it was my turn to be the face of the carol singers as a new door opened to hopefully greet us.  The gentleman who opened the door, looked at me, looked at those around me, looked back at me, his eyes widened and he said, 'Peter, what are you doing?' In a rush it dawned on me that Mr B had been the Chairman of an advertising agency to which I had been appointed Liquidator a week or so prior.  He was himself Jewish, was referred to us by firms of Jewish solicitors and accountants and who had, maybe not unreasonably, made assumptions about what I did and didn't do in my private life.

I can't actually remember whether he donated to the carol singers but I never saw him again.


**Accountants** – *'People can tell stories about accountants and say whatever they think about them and still be politically correct.'*

With David Marks QC at the Grand Canyon, October 2004

## Helicopters are Dangerous

We sometimes think that accidents don't happen to us and take certain risks that if we thought about it more, we would not take. I can't complain, but much of my professional work came about because individuals have taken just one risk too many.

Just before I retired, I was at an international insolvency conference in Las Vegas, when with a few colleagues we decided to take the helicopter trip over and into the Grand Canyon. The picture shows David Marks QC, an eminent insolvency lawyer, and myself, in the Canyon itself.

When we returned to the conference we met a lot of anxious faces relieved to see we had returned in one piece as another helicopter that had gone out at the same time had crashed, killing all on board.

"SOME SAY LIQUIDATION DROVE HIM TO DRINK, OTHERS SAY DRINK DROVE HIM INTO LIQUIDATION"

P. Sheen

## Some have Greatness Thrust upon Them!

One of the more interesting aspects of insolvency practice has been representation of creditors at creditors meetings when companies are being liquidated and Liquidators need to be appointed.  Whilst the shareholders make the initial decision to appoint a Liquidator, and whom that should be, the creditors have the right, if they so exercise it, to appoint a Liquidator of their choice.  Not surprisingly the decision is driven by the value of creditors claims supporting any particular nomination.

In the early 1980s I had just attended a meeting of creditors in the vast offices of the then Department of the Official Receivers and I had conducted myself in the time honoured manner of asking the Chairman of the meeting key questions that might determine whether or not those I was representing should seek to appoint their own Liquidator.  As it happened, on that particular occasion, that was not necessary.

I left the meeting and was walking down one of the many corridors of the very old-fashioned building when I saw walking towards me a large group of people, a number of whom I recognised as professional competitors.

We greeted each other, they asked where I was going, and jokingly suggested I was going the wrong direction.  I, obligingly, changed direction and followed them into another meeting of creditors which was about to commence.

Before I had time to absent myself from a meeting to which I had not been invited, a number of other creditors representatives assuming I was there myself representing a creditor, indicated, without prompting, that if I would like their support as the nominated liquidator they would be pleased to give it to me.

I was troubled. First of all I had not been invited to the meeting and should really have left, but secondly competitors are not normally charitable to each other. Therefore, for what was I being set up?

I made a 'management decision' and stayed in my seat to hear the long and convoluted report from the Chairman of the meeting. As the situation, on the one hand, became clearer but, on the other hand, more opaque, a number of creditors representatives decided they had heard enough and left the meeting to move onto other matters.

As they left, some of them gave me their voting rights to be exercised later in the meeting. By the time it came to the nomination of a Liquidator it became clear that no one was really interested in taking on a case with thousands of creditors which was already in Receivership and where the Receivers could not give any clear indication that there would be funds left over for creditors when the Receivers had finished their job for the bank.

I just had that sort feeling, as they say, that the creditors would be well advised to appoint their own Liquidator. Entirely by default I agreed to take on the liquidation which at the time was no doubt a relief in the minds of those nominating me.

The case turned out to be very much more complicated than even those attending the meeting suspected, but the Receivers did an exceptional job of selling the business assets. The extraordinary end to this tale is that some twelve or thirteen years later I had sufficient monies in my hands to pay all creditors, who totalled between £10-20 million, approximately 98p in the pound.

I suppose the only business lesson I can draw from this story is the value of being in the right place at the right time, albeit, I was in the wrong place at the right time. It's all a question of perspective.

Life After Debt

*Evening Standard* – 15th August 1991
Paul Thomas

# Computers

This is a little tale of confession and evolution.

Elsewhere I talked about my early years at Arthur Andersen and of the assistance I was given with computerised presentations. When I was thinking about my exposure to the high-tech world it dawned on me that I, perhaps in more than one respect, was a slightly unorthodox partner at Andersen's. When I was admitted as a partner and installed in a beautiful office with a view over the Thames near Waterloo Bridge, it was garnished with a wonderful tall potted palm tree and a computer was plonked on my desk.

I find it bizarre now to acknowledge that in the entire time I spent in that office between 1982 and 1988 I never once turned the computer on, and probably would have needed help to be able to turn it on in the first place.

I did not however remain a complete dodo as on leaving Andersen's and joining David Buchler to form Buchler Phillips we decided that, our then tiny practice of less than a dozen people, would, from the off, be an integrated network with a PC on everybody's desk. Strange as it may sound, in 1988 this was pioneering stuff. We were in fact the first insolvency practice in the United Kingdom to operate in this way and as we grew many other insolvency practices, including a number of the Big Four accounting firms came to review our approach and systems. In many cases they adopted them as quickly as possible, with our agreement, encouragement and satisfaction.

## Is it Me, my Beard, or my Silly Walk?

For much of my life I have been plagued with people telling me how much I remind them of John Cleese. This is not necessarily a compliment and on occasions I have sensed it has not merely been a reference to my physical appearance. In an attempt to break this cycle many years ago I grew a beard. Shortly afterwards Mr Cleese grew a beard which meant, of course, that people continued to insist on how much I resembled him.

David Buchler (see other tales) really enjoyed the impact this had on those who met us and took particular advantage of it when we were both working on the Interkiln case. (see page xx)

You may remember that Interkiln was a company owned by a German State Authority and this required us to make regular reporting visits to, what was then, Eastern Germany.

In those days it was impossible to fly direct from London into Berlin, the then capital of Eastern Germany. One had to fly British Airways to a Western German airport and then board a German airline into Berlin. On one of these trips David and I were sitting behind each other in the (please note) Economy section of the plane when I noticed one of the stewardesses chatting earnestly to him. I mistakenly assumed that David's charms were working as effectively as usual, until I noticed that I was receiving extra special attention from the crew. This continued throughout the flight and right down the steps into the airport back at London.

# Life After Debt

When we were clear of the airport David asked me whether
I had wondered why I was being treated so well on the plane?
I said, I did. He informed me that he had been asked by the
stewardess whether his friend, i.e. Me, was John Cleese and he
had confirmed that she was right.

**Comedians** – *'Some accountants are comedians, but comedians
are never accountants.'*

George Carman QC, at the trial of Ken Dodd on alleged tax
evasion.

## Mad Dogs and ... (Part 1)

In an earlier episode I talked about an entertaining evening in Hong Kong with one of my former partners.  This one is about an entertaining midday, on the same island, with another of my former partners, Simon Freakley.

This particular year, Simon and I had agreed to make presentations to the financial community in Hong Kong.  The stay on that island was made even more exciting than usual as I had been invited by Jardine Matheson, a global corporation which had a major involvement in the development of the colony of Hong Kong, to fire the Noonday Gun as their guest.

The Noonday Gun is a former naval gun mounted on a small enclosed site near the Causeway Bay typhoon shelter where it has been since the 1860s.  For at least a hundred years it has been fired at noon every day to serve as a time signal.  Although British rule ended in Hong Kong in 1997 the Noonday Gun is continued by Jardines in perpetuity.  It is a tourist attraction and junks carrying visitors gather daily to watch the ceremony. I considered the invitation I had received a great honour as a number of those who wanted to perform this ceremony paid significant sums for the privilege.

Anyway, my great day came, not surprisingly I wanted to immortalise it and had taken my camcorder.  No less importantly I had taken, my then partner, Simon Freakley, who kindly agreed to act as camera man.  The event went entirely to plan with the small exception that as I pulled, under naval instructions, the cord that fired the cannon, it let out such retort that dear Simon dropped the camera catching it before it hit the ground.

When I am able to bore members of the family with films of my exploits this is one of the more entertaining.

## Mad Dogs and ... (Part 2)

In the 1980s Arthur Andersen gave me responsibility for supervising the insolvency work being done in its office in Hong Kong. This required me to go out there every two months to review the case files and make contact with key clients.

On my first visit I was delivered to the Mandarin Hotel after, what in those days, was a very long two-part flight, at breakfast time their local time. As the lift doors opened for me to go up to my room, standing facing me, coming out of the lift, was someone I knew very well indeed, as the senior insolvency partner of the excellent UK practice then known as Thornton Baker, more recently Grant Thornton. My old friend and competitor, Douglas Corkish, could not believe his eyes when he saw me and asked what I was doing there. I told him I was about to take on some very large banking failures and asked him to explain his own presence. His answer was much more interesting. He, I had known for a long time, was the Chairman of Liverpool Football Club and he was with his team on a tour of friendlies, one of which was being held that weekend on Hong Kong Island.

Without my asking, he immediately said, 'I will have two tickets waiting for you at the players' entrance, bear in mind you'll have to dress up smart'. I felt very pleased with myself when I walked into the Andersen office and told my then resident insolvency senior manager and subsequent Buchler Phillips partner, Ted Wacey, what he and I would be doing that Saturday afternoon.

# Life After Debt

We worked that Saturday morning, as everybody, in those days and may still work on Hong Kong Island, and took a taxi to Happy Valley, where the match was to be held.  We strolled confidently to what looked like the main gates and the main entrance but couldn't see the players' entrance clearly marked anywhere.  We asked for directions and were directed round the stadium.  We followed our directions and, after what seemed like quite a long time, came to an unprepossessing set of turnstiles at what were clearly the terraces, headed Players' Entrance.  We walked in and found ourselves in an absolutely packed terrace, but packed with locals dressed in little more than swimming costumes, whilst we were there in working clothes, in those days, dark suits, white shirts and ties.

We spent the next two hours enjoying the match and boiling to death.  It would have made a wonderful photograph if someone had seen us.

A couple of days later Douglas Corkish rang to ask how we enjoyed ourselves and when I explained what had happened his embarrassment was evident.  He had had no idea what had gone wrong but in partial compensation he took me the following year to the FA Cup final at Wembley, London.

## Annabelle's, Armani - a Record?

My former partner, Simon Freakley, the cameraman in an earlier chapter, has been a very important figure in my professional career. He is another of the very gifted fellow practitioners that I have had the fortune of either working in partnership with or in competition with over my career. He eventually became Worldwide President of Kroll, the company that took over Buchler Phillips and now chairs Zolfo Cooper.

However, well before we were even approached by Kroll, the partners of Buchler Phillips used to arrange a major client event annually, at the Savoy Hotel in London, when up to 400 great and good would be invited to participate in a private version of the famous programme *Question Time*. My firm would invite four well known public figures to debate questions of the day in front of and with the audience. Although the last of these was held over ten years ago, former business associates still remind me that they regarded those evenings as the high spot of the professional social calendar.

Although, those evenings would end at ten o'clock, for the then young and spirited partner and manager group of Buchler Phillips, the evening was just beginning. I thought I would extend festivities for those of my staff who had worked hard with the partners to arrange the evening, together with some selected guests from the evening to come to Annabelle's with me. We spoke to the doorman and explained that a number of guests would be coming along, but I was not quite sure later on whether I was quite so happy, when was told that I had broken the record for guests and something in excess of sixty had followed me as the small hours approached. Even later in the evening I was asked if I could deal with a problem being caused by two of my guests who I would find in the gentlemen's cloakroom. I was not sure what I would encounter but I walked into the cloakroom to find that Andrew Duncan, one of my antipodean managers, as a response to a little too much of the amber nectar, had disgorged his evenings consumption over poor Simon Freakley. Simon's personal distress was not least occasioned by the fact that he was wearing an Armani suit that he had only bought that week. It was clear that a management decision was needed and I invited Andy and Simon to go home.

## Sir Richard Harford

Marketing can take many forms, but one of the most idiosyncratic and appealing examples of subliminal marketing is the subject of this little story.

In the late 1960s a couple of fellow practitioners decided to set up their own practice in the West End of London and proudly announced their opening with an invitation to a function at the practice that bore the name Richard Harford & Co.

I duly went along to the drinks party and admired the very large and beautifully framed oil painting in the Board Room, who was, as indicated below it, Sir Richard Harford.  Some while later I thought I would ask one of the partners what the relevance to the practice was of Sir Richard Harford and was delighted to be told, nothing at all.  The partners had seen the oil painting in an auction, had bought it, put it on the wall and named their practice after it.

# Who Remembers Stamp Duty?

In 1918 the Stamp Duty on cheques was increased from 1d to 2d. The old Stamp Duty had been signified by an oval stamp, whilst the new Stamp Duty was signified by a new 2d duty stamp.

What this meant was that when one was issued with a cheque book one had to pay 2d for every cheque in it.

In the early 70s the Phillips' office was handling many hundreds of separate trust bank accounts for the creditors of the various companies in liquidation that we were managing. That meant, of course, that in our offices were many hundreds of cheque books being used on those bank accounts.

One day Percy called Bernard and me into his office where, with a smile on his face, he proudly told us that he had saved the office some money.  What this was all about was that, in around the early 70s the government abolished Stamp Duty on cheque books and agreed to credit people with the 2d per cheque on any unused cheques returned to their banks.  Percy, ever careful with his pennies, had culled all unused cheques from the office.  These he had then sent to the bank for due credit.

When everything was totted up the money credited was less than £40, but the cull had not merely sent to the shredder at the bank the unused cheques, but the cheque stubs from the used cheques as well.  This meant that the cash records for all the accounts we were running could not be written up and I dread to think the cost in man hours for what one got in those days, namely the returned cheques though the banking system, to then recreate the cash records.

# Maxwell

*'You are as safe with me as you would be with the Bank of England.'*

Robert Maxwell

## Maxwell

Very few of you should need reminding of how much interest the demise of Robert Maxwell stirred up in the early 1990s.

For those of you who would like to find out rather more than what I tell you about in the next few pages may I strongly recommend the Tom Bower book on Maxwell. I was one of the many people Tom Bower interviewed for his book and it was therefore more than a little ironic that on my fiftieth birthday in 1994, one of my closest friends gave me a parcel which I eagerly unwrapped. Inside was a copy of the Bower book which had been hollowed out and inside it placed a delightful Asprey leather wallet with my initials on it.

# THE ESTATE OF THE LATE IAN ROBERT MAXWELL

Pursuant to an Order of the High Court of Justice in England and Wales dated 16 December 1991, Ian Peter Phillips, David Julian Buchler and Edward John Wacey, all of Buchler Phillips & Co., were appointed Joint Receivers of the Estate of the late Ian Robert Maxwell.

The Receivers' mandate is to identify and gather in all assets belonging to the late Ian Robert Maxwell. Accordingly, the Receivers would like to hear from any person who has any information or knowledge, which may be of assistance in ascertaining the full particulars of all assets, situated both within or outside the United Kingdom, held by or on behalf of the late Ian Robert Maxwell, or to which his Estate may be beneficially entitled. Anyone with such information or who may be able to be of assistance to the Receivers in performing their tasks is requested to contact Peter Phillips, Derek Wilson or Gerard Goodwyn at:–

Buchler Phillips & Co.,
84 Grosvenor Street
London W1X 9DF
Telephone 071-493 2550
Facsimile 071-629 9444

*Financial Times* – January 14th 1992

# Robert Maxwell (Deceased)

Without any doubt the most demanding case I have handled in my career was the Court Receivership (see glossary) of the late Robert Maxwell.

Enough has already been written about this gentleman, whom I in fact, never met, for me to happily limit my recollections to those arising out of my efforts to deal with his assets after his death. I have no intention of expressing any personal views about his alleged conduct. I should perhaps muse wistfully at the fact that at one stage of the work that I was handling, it seemed to me that I was receiving more opprobrium for the alleged cost of my work than Robert Maxwell was receiving for the alleged cost of his. Even Kevin, his son, once commented to me that it seemed that the Press was giving me 'more grief' than him!

Although people tend to recognise the question, 'What were you doing on the night President Kennedy died?' I find it much easier to remember what I was doing on the day that Robert Maxwell disappeared, i.e. 5th November 1991.

I was in New York with David Buchler and our affiliate Stuart Kahn, Chairman of Kahn Consulting, in their offices near Central Park. David, Stuart and I held annual seminars at one of the recital rooms at Carnegie Hall for lawyers, accountants and bankers to come and hear debated issues of relevance to the insolvency and bankruptcy professional communities. A lot of hard work used to go into these events and about three or four hours before the November 1991 event was due to commence our preparations were interrupted by someone with the news they had received that Robert Maxwell had gone missing.

I very clearly remember asking myself, and then sharing with my colleagues, the question, 'I wonder if we're going to find ourselves involved professionally in this crisis?'

Relatively shortly after my return to the United Kingdom, I was telephoned by solicitors representing Mirror Group Newspapers, and asked if I would consent to be nominated in a court application as Receiver of the estate of the late Robert Maxwell.

Answering 'yes' was the easiest part of a long tortuous assignment.

**Neutron Loan** – *'The neutron loan is a secured advance made to a borrower who fails after which the lender also fails, but the security remains intact.'*

# The Irony

The directions set out in the Application granted by the Court were, that I be appointed Joint Receiver to identify, seek out and protect all assets belonging to the late Robert Maxwell anywhere in the world.

The case took a lot of time and a lot of work. I, in fact, only applied for my release as Receiver from the Court (and obtained it) in 2005, some thirteen years later. For those truly interested or ignorant of the enormous interest taken in my work, or rather the cost of it, by both the judge supervising it and Frank Field, as Chairman of House of Commons Social Security Select Committee there is more than enough material in the public domain to satisfy that curiosity.

There is, maybe inevitably, little in the public domain, except for one article entitled 'The Recovery Position' by Jim Kelly in the *Financial Times* for the 22nd April 1999 explaining how this was eventually concluded.

> Buchler Phillips, the accountancy firm, has won a footnote in the history of insolvency. At one time it looked like being an infamous one. The firm, acting as receivers, had tried to track down the personal assets of Robert Maxwell. This had cost £1.6m – against asset recoveries to date of £1.7m. Mr Justice Ferris, called on to review the costs, felt that a system that produced this kind of result was 'profoundly shocking' and 'deeply shameful'.
>
> Justice Ferris passed the issue to Master Hurst, a 'taxing officer' (an official expert at evaluating professional fees), and last week delivered his judgement. He awarded Buchler Phillips £659,259.50p – 99 per cent of their claim for fees of £666,000 – and found no wrongdoing in its conduct. The firm

is completely vindicated.  The jury – so to speak – is still out on the system that produced such a result.

The taxing master laid the blame on the way Mr Maxwell had organised his business: 'Many assets which on the face of it appeared to be the personal property of Mr Maxwell were either worthless or, because of the immensely complex financial labyrinth which he had constructed, could not ultimately be recovered as personal property.'

Put, as QCs say, shortly, a full independent judicial scrutiny of my work and my proposed fees resulted in a fifty-six page judgement complimenting me on the work I had done and awarding me 99.6% of the fees I sought.

Having got that out of the way, those still here should enjoy the following five stories.  These have unfailingly produced gasps when I have told them on my professional travels.

# Lichtenstein

Lichtenstein has a particular cachet for those interested in the world of opaque wealth.  Those of you readers who have visited it will know that it looks about as close to one's fantasy of what somewhere called Lichtenstein could appear as it could possibly be.

It is a dark towering gothic town nestling off the main railway line between Zurich and the Swiss Alps.  It has as its principal, if not only, attraction many, many banks within which are contained an undisclosed number of private safe deposit boxes. One of these, it was discovered in the course of my enquiries, belonged to Robert Maxwell.

In the very early days of the collapse of the Maxwell empire, when there were three major accounting firms, in addition to my own, as well as at least as many legal firms, wrestling with the massive challenges of this complex corporate and personal empire, there was a widely held assumption that the mystery of the missing millions or the mystery of the black hole in the pension funds, would largely be solved if only the secrecy laws in Switzerland and Lichtenstein could be by-passed.

This book, being a collection of short stories, is not the place to provide a technical lecture on the many issues raised by the banking practices of Switzerland and Lichtenstein.  The point of this episode is that I was eventually successful in obtaining permission to personally visit Lichtenstein and personally open, what was discovered to be, the safe deposit box of the late Robert Maxwell.

# Life After Debt

As you may well imagine, there was considerable excitement at the prospect of this visit and I found myself accompanied by not only my own solicitor, Peter Sigler, of Nabarro Nathanson in London, but a Lichtenstein lawyer who advised us throughout on the complexities of the world we were dealing with over there.

I remember the day very well. I was not merely apprehensive, but pleased that in the cost conscious environment in which everybody was operating, I was going to be able to do what I had to do in one day, namely travel from London to Lichtenstein and back, Economy as usual.

Everything went to plan, and by lunchtime we found ourselves taking the strange little bus that goes from the railway line in Switzerland into Vaduz in Lichtenstein.

We entered one of the dozens of similar looking banking establishments in the high street and were escorted down into a massive safe deposit. One of the executives of the bank walked us to where Maxwell's box was amongst hundreds of others. He and I produced our respective keys and we opened the outer hinged door. I looked inside and, yes, there was the box. I had no way of predicting what was going to be found in it, but certainly amongst the various possibilities, what actually was found, was not on my list of possibilities.

I took the box to a nearby table and we eagerly surrounded it, whilst I put the key in it and opened the lid.

We craned our necks and looked in and discovered... a rubber band! And nothing else...

# Life After Debt

A number of us, of course, were extremely clever after the event, asserting that we were surprised even to find a rubber band.

It still however strikes me as more than a little strange that by simply a coincidence in timing, Robert Maxwell disappeared, was pronounced dead, his empire collapsed and his safe deposit box was empty.

*Evening Standard* – 11th July 1997
Paul Thomas

## M'Nuts, M'Lud

In mid December 1991 the title of this chapter was the headline in one of the UK's favourite tabloid newspapers. In that journal's inimitable style it was an idiosyncratic perspective of an extraordinary incident that had taken place the previous week.

The background to this story is that one of the other insolvency practitioners dealing with key aspects of the Maxwell empire was Neil Cooper, then of Robson Rhodes, and latterly an ex-partner of mine at Kroll. He had been appointed provisional Liquidator (see glossary) of Bishopsgate Investment Management Ltd, the company managing the Maxwell pension scheme.

On 8th December 1991, through an ex-parte application (see glossary) Neil had obtained various Orders from the High Court, one being that Kevin and Ian Maxwell surrender their passports. On 9th December when the Maxwell brothers were made aware of the Court Order they made an application for that order to be reversed. Their application was an emergency application to be heard in the evening. That required the Judge, the Duty Judge at the time, the Honourable Mr Justice Harman, to be collected from his home by taxi, to enable him to consider the application.

In the ways that the Press find out about exciting events, the Press found out that this was going on and as Mr Justice Harman left his home at night time he was met and dazzled by an array of paparazzi and their flash lights.

Presumably somewhat disoriented, it is clear that he felt under threat from a powerfully built man in a leather jacket purposefully walking towards him.  Mr Justice Harman was in no mood to be anybody's victim and presumably, deciding that the best form of defence was attack, put all his weight behind a kick that landed at the top and the centre of the apparent assailants own legs.  As the Judge was preparing for a second shot, and it is not clear whether the words he then heard were falsetto, his victim said something to the effect that, as a taxi driver he should be given a break as he was only trying to take the judge to Court.

The paparazzi meanwhile were enjoying a far more valuable scoop than they could ever have anticipated.

What seems to be clear now though is that for some days, indeed for the better part of a week, no newspaper felt brave enough to report this eye-watering incident.  Finally, however, the immortal headlines referred to and heading this chapter, accompanied by a photograph of the moment of contact did appear, providing one of the very few moments of light relief during the Maxwell empire's collapse and unravelling.

## Just one of Those Things?

Amongst the very basic tasks that my team were engaged in at the beginning of the case was to analyse Robert Maxwell's personal bank statements and investigate any odd or material transactions.  The detailed results of our work were supplied to the Court and are not going to be reproduced here.

The point of this story is that whilst scouring his personal bank statements we discovered that a standing order had been established a few months before Robert Maxwell's death in favour of the Banbury Sub Aqua Club.

We never found out why.

# Life After Debt

'The thing I would like to see invented is a way of teaching children and grown-ups the difference between right and wrong.'

Robert Maxwell

## Another Irony?

Shortly after I took office I was telephoned by a professor at Southampton University, who, having introduced himself, explained that Robert Maxwell had bestowed a research grant on the University for three years. The professor understandably wished to know whether the second and third instalments would be received as promised.

Even at that very early stage, it had become clear to most people, that if any assets were ever found belonging to Maxwell, then the estimated hundreds of millions of pounds lost by the empire would make short work of those.

Before concluding the conversation and assuring the professor that if the position changed materially I would of course inform him, I asked what the research project that Maxwell had funded had been. I was stunned to be told that the project was maritime safety and research.

For those on whom any irony has been lost, it has been generally accepted that Robert Maxwell died having left his yacht, the *Lady Ghislaine* in the Atlantic Ocean. Much has been said about falling, pushing and jumping and I do not wish to reopen those discussions further.

Having said that my final Maxwell story may inevitably, stimulate fantasies about other possibilities.

# STILL WAITING

## United in the dark over new owners

By JON MURRAY

THE new owners of Oxford United should be known by Easter.

Peter Phillips of the receivers for the estate of the late Robert Maxwell told shareholders last night that he had received four offers for the club — but he wouldn't accept any of them.

However, after the re-convened AGM was over, Phillips put his own estimate on how long it would take him to sell the shares.

### Talking

"It's definitely weeks rather than days," he said, "and it should be wrapped up in a month."

The receivers had hoped to be able to reveal the buyers at the annual meeting, which had been adjourned from March 5, but they had not had enough time.

"I have been engaged in detailed discussions and at this moment in time I have had four firm, detailed and very interesting offers. However, I do not find inclined to accept any of them," the receiver told shareholders.

It's believed negoti-

ations with prospective buyers have also involved discussions on whether the £1.8 million loan made by Kevin Maxwell to United should be excluded from any offer.

"There is more hard talking to be done," said Phillips.

Yet United's managing director Pat McGeough was annoyed that the receivers have taken so long to sort out the best bid.

"Today's meeting gives me very little encouragement," he said. "The interest he serves the club. The fact that they keep extending the deadline is to the detriment of Oxford United.

"We've got a period of uncertainty again and the fact that it's beyond our control is infuriating."

United now face a big dilemma: to sell or not to sell one of their play-ers before Thursday's transfer deadline.

They need to sell another player before the end of the season to be able to pay the players' wages — unless there is help either from Nat-West Bank, or in the

form of new owners coming in with cash.

The dilemma comes with the fact that they don't know who the new owners will be, nor whether they will offer the cash up front to avoid having to sell a player.

And if a player has to be sold, that really needs to be done by 5pm on Thursday.

### Asset

Manager Brian Horton revealed at the weekend that he had turned down a bid last week for Joey Beauchamp, who is probably United's most saleable asset.

But after last night's AGM, receiver Phillips said privately that United knew the offers he had received were serious ones, and they could surely hold fire with the sale likely to go through soon.

"It's not as though we're not in contact with the club," he said.

A fuller explanation of the mystery £1.8 million loan from Maxwell to United was sought at the original AGM and last night chartered accountants Critchleys confirmed they were now satisfied with the terms of the loan.

Receiver Peter Phillips (left) and chairman Kevin Maxwell at last night's meeting

### BACK PAGE COMMENT

## Receivers must get on with it

By THE EDITOR

THE receivers dealing with the affairs of Oxford United should get their game plan together.

Last night's prediction that it will take another two to three weeks to formalise the new ownership is no good to a club fighting against relegation.

The receivers should take another look at the way the players are fighting back, and the tremendous spirit of United's supporters.

They should copy this effort, get on with ratifying the best bid, and help the club stay in the second division.

And that needs to be done now, not two or three weeks' time.

## Maxwell stays — for now

SHAREHOLDERS did not want Kevin Maxwell to remain as chairman at last night's AGM but he will anyway — at least until the club has a new owner thanks to the weight of his own shares, writes JON MURRAY.

Maxwell said he was "personally happy to remain as chairman of the company".

In accordance with the Articles of Associa-

*Oxford Mail* – 24th March 1992

## Oxford United

One of the very few material assets I found for the Court where ownership was clear was the controlling shareholding Robert Maxwell had personally in Oxford United Football Club. At the time of the commencement of the Receivership, the Club was struggling at the foot of the old Second Division of the Football League (now the Championship). Kevin Maxwell was its Chairman, and another individual was its Manager. My team reviewed the health of the Club, and interviewed the Chairman and Manager separately.

Kevin Maxwell's opinion was that it would be in the best financial interests of the receivership for the Club to sell its players, albeit that might inevitably result in the Club's relegation.

The Manager, unsurprisingly, took the very opposite position, prioritising the survival of the Club. As if that were not an interesting enough challenge, the most pressing issue, for me, was the imminent Annual General Meeting and the re-appointment of the company's officers. As Maxwell's Receiver I stepped into his shoes as owner of the Club with the right to appoint and remove any directors I wanted. The choices though, facing me, were limited. I could remove Kevin Maxwell and allow myself to be placed in the position of caretaker Chairman and Director or leave the position with Kevin Maxwell, the Chairman of the Club, whilst facing the glare of publicity and opprobrium, justified or unjustified, from the entire British public.

It was clear to me and I was so advised by my solicitor, that it was not appropriate for me to join the company as its

Chairman, whilst it was in such a bad way. It seemed preferable for every effort to be made to find a purchaser for the club. In which case, if Kevin Maxwell could be persuaded to stay in place, properly monitored, that should work. And in fact it did...

The Annual General Meeting was attended by a posse of media and I am pretty sure I was the only person to have appointed (or rather re-appointed) Kevin Maxwell to any company after his father's death for many years.

Several more extraordinary meetings took place, attended by hordes of supporters and reporters, which effectively were chaired by both myself informally and Kevin formally.

The eventual sale of the Club took an extremely long time and was a very complicated process. I remember completing the transaction one evening in a large West End hotel, shortly after Oxford United had played their last game of the season and had saved themselves from relegation.

The following week the Oxford United Supporters Club invited me to go and join them for a cup of tea at the ground. I duly turned up to meet a relatively small group of long-standing, unsophisticated and forthright supporters.

They wanted to thank me for, as they saw it, saving their Club and it was very nice indeed to be thanked for anything in those days. We had a cup of tea and a few biscuits and made small talk until one of them started being less than complimentary about Robert Maxwell. The sorts of things that were being said were that he had never really done anything for the Club. I was not in a position to comment, as I had not been around at the time that it certainly seemed that he was doing things for the Club. I did remind them that the Press often carried photographs of him sitting in the Directors' box for the home matches. This I said, in all innocence, and was stunned to hear a number of supporters seeking to *put me right*.

What they said was, 'That wasn't Maxwell, it was his double, everybody knew that there was a middle European double that sat in the Directors' box, therefore there was no point in going up and complaining to him as he didn't speak any English'.

All I can tell you is what I heard. What you make of it will have to be up to you.

# Vindication and a Smile - The OBE

With Kira, Wendy and Leo outside Buckingham Palace,
February 2004

## Vindication and a Smile – the OBE

As may now be appreciated I have had a lot of pleasure from my professional career, but also not a few major challenges. The Press appears to have usually held the insolvency professional in low regard and other professions have been reluctant to acknowledge the distinct professional status of those doing the work I did for forty years. Last but not least the savaging I received from both the House of Commons Social Security Select Committee under Frank Field and the Press over the Maxwell case is an experience I would not recommend to anyone without health insurance and a compassionate wife! (The former has already come in very useful!)

You will understand therefore the delight and astonishment I experienced when I opened a letter in mid-November 2003, informing me that the Prime Minister had it in mind to recommend to the Queen, that I be honoured as OBE for Services to the insolvency profession.

On a day early in the 2004 after my award had been made public I, together with others being honoured and their families attended Buckingham Palace to be presented to her Majesty the Queen.

After brief and comprehensive training in the protocols of the event each of us was presented individually to Her Majesty. When it was my turn to step forward and to shake her hand she addressed a few words to me.

She enquired whether I ever found the work I did depressing? I responded by explaining that I preferred to look at the work

# Life After Debt

I did as a little like that carried out by a doctor who can repair the health of some of his patients and relieve the suffering of others.  Her Majesty nodded cautiously saying she understood.

I could have left it like that but I felt constrained to add, 'Ma'am, I have to say that not everybody sees it that way', to which she responded with a big smile, 'I imagine they don't!'

When I rejoined my family after the ceremony they were fascinated to know how I had managed, as they saw it, to make the Queen laugh.

# Glossary And Index

*Daily Mail* – 17 February 1982

# Glossary

Some of the terms I have used, may not be familiar to everybody.

So I have added a list to help readers.

These are with thanks to R3, the trade body of the insolvency industry in the UK.  See www.r3.org.uk for more details of the organisation.

**Administration** – Administration is a process which places a company under the control of a Licensed Insolvency Practitioner and the protection of the court to achieve a specified statutory purpose. The purpose of administration is to save the company, or if that is not possible, to achieve a better result for creditors than in a liquidation, or if neither of those is possible, to realise property to enable funds to be distributed to secured or preferential creditors.

**Administration Order** – An administration order is:
1. A court order placing a company that is, or is likely to become, insolvent under the control of an administrator in order to achieve the purpose of administration, following a petition by the company, its directors, its liquidator or a creditor.
2. The administration of the insolvent estate of a deceased debtor
3. County Court process permitting an individual with modest debts to pay off by instalments; no Licensed Insolvency Practitioner is involved.

**Administrative Receiver** – An administrative receiver is a Licensed Insolvency Practitioner appointed by the holder of a floating charge covering the whole, or substantially the whole, of a company's property. They can carry on the company's business and sell the business and other assets comprised in the charge to repay the secured and preferential creditors. This is sometimes abbreviated to receiver.

**Administrative Receivership** – Administrative receivership is the term applied when a person is appointed as an administrative receiver.  This is commonly abbreviated to receivership.

**Administrator** – An administrator is a Licensed Insolvency Practitioner  appointed to manage the affairs of a company to achieve the purpose of administration set out in the Insolvency Act 1986.  The administrator will need to produce a plan, known as his proposals, for approval by the creditors to achieve this.

**Agricultural Receivership** – Agricultural receivership is a specialist remedy available to a secured creditor to take control of the assets of a farmer under the Agricultural Credits Act 1928.

**Annulment** – Cancellation.

**Assets** – Anything that belongs to the debtor that may be used to pay his/her debts.

**Associates** – Associates of individuals include family members, relatives, partners and their relatives, employees, employers, trustees in certain trust relationships, and companies which the individual controls. Associates of companies include other companies under common control (see also connected persons).

**Bankrupt** – A bankrupt is an individual against whom a bankruptcy order has been made by the court. The order signifies that the individual is unable to pay his/her debts and deprives him/her of his/her property, which is then realised for distribution amongst his creditors.

**Bankruptcy** – Bankruptcy is the process of dealing with the estate of a bankrupt.

**Bankruptcy Restrictions Order Or Undertaking** – A procedure will be introduced on 1 April 2004 whereby a bankrupt who has been dishonest or in some other way to blame for their bankruptcy may have a court order made against them or give an undertaking to the Secretary of State which will mean that bankruptcy restrictions continue to apply after discharge for a period of between two to fifteen years.

**Bond** – A bond is Insurance cover to protect the uncharged assets of an estate, needed by a person who acts as a Licensed Insolvency Practitioner .

**Break-up Sale** – A break-up sale is the dismantling of a business. Trading ceases and the assets are sold off piecemeal.

**Charge** – A charge is a right given to the creditor to have a designated asset of the debtor appropriated to the discharge of the indebtedness, but not involving any transfer either of possession or ownership.

**Charging Order** – A charging order is a court order placing restrictions on the disposal of certain assets, such as property or securities, given after judgement and gives priority of payment over other creditors.

**Company Directors Disqualification Act 1986** – The Company Directors Disqualification Act 1986 is an act concerning the disqualification of persons from being directors or otherwise concerned with a company's affairs.

**Company Voluntary Arrangement (CVA)** - A company voluntary arrangement is a voluntary arrangement for a company is a procedure whereby a plan of reorganisation or composition in satisfaction of its debts is put forward to creditors and shareholders. There is limited involvement by the court and the scheme is under the control of a supervisor.

**Composition** - A composition is an agreement between a debtor and his creditors whereby the compounding creditors agree with the debtor and between themselves to accept from the debtor payment of less than the amounts due to them in full satisfaction of their claim.

**Compulsory Liquidation** - A compulsory liquidation of a company is a liquidation ordered by the court. This is usually as a result of a petition presented to the court by a creditor and is the only method by which a creditor can bring about a liquidation of its debtor company.

**Connected Persons** - Connected persons are directors or shadow directors and their associates, and associates of a company.

**Contributory** - Every person liable to contribute to the assets of a company if it is wound up. In most cases this means shareholders who have not paid for their shares in full.

**Cork Report** - The Report of the Insolvency Law Review Committee, chaired by Sir Kenneth Cork, upon which the Insolvency Act 1986 is substantially based (Command Paper 8555, 1982).

**Court-appointed Receiver** – A court-appointed receiver is a person, not necessarily a Licensed Insolvency Practitioner , appointed to take charge of assets usually where they are subject to some legal dispute.  Not strictly an insolvency process, the procedure may be used other than for a limited company, e.g. to settle a partnership dispute.

**Creditor** – Someone owed money by a bankrupt or company.

**Creditors' Committee** – A creditors' committee is a committee formed to represent the interests of all creditors in administrations, administrative receiverships and bankruptcies. The exact functions of the Committee depend on the type of procedure (c.f. Liquidation Committee).

**Creditors' Voluntary Liquidation (CVL)** – A creditors' voluntary liquidation relates to an insolvent company.  It is commenced by resolution of the shareholders, but is under the effective control of creditors, who can choose the liquidator.

**Debenture** – A debenture, broadly speaking, a document which either acknowledges or creates a debt.  The expression is commonly used to denote a document conferring a fixed and floating charge over all the assets and undertakings of a company.

**Deed of Arrangement** – A deed of arrangement is a method for an individual (not a company) to come to terms with creditors outside formal bankruptcy. The procedure is governed by the Deeds of Arrangement Act 1914 and is now almost completely replaced by voluntary arrangements.

**Director** – A person who conducts the affairs of a company.

**Disqualification of Directors** – A director found to have conducted the affairs of an insolvent company in an 'unfit' manner will be disqualified, on application to the court by the DTI, from holding any management position in a company for between two and 15 years.

**Dividend** – Any sum distributed to unsecured creditors in an insolvency.

**Ex-Parte Application** – This is an application to the Court made without notice or opportunity to oppose.

**Extortionate Credit Transaction** – An extortionate credit transaction is a transaction by which credit is provided on terms that are exorbitant or grossly unfair compared with the risk accepted by the creditor. Such a transaction may be challenged by an administrator, a liquidator or a trustee in bankruptcy.

**Financial Services Compensation Scheme** – The Financial Services Compensation Scheme was established under the Financial Services and Markets Act 2000 to provide compensation for certain claims in the event of the default of a regulated financial services business. From 1 December 2001 it replaced the previous compensation schemes for investment business, banking, building societies and insurance. The maximum levels of compensation are:

1. Deposits – 100% of the first £50,000.
2. Investments – 100% of the first £30,000, 90% of the next £20,000.
3. Insurance – 100% of the first £2,000, 90% of the remainder of claim or value. Claims under certain policies of the compulsory insurance are paid in full.

**Fixed Charge** – A fixed charge is a form of security granted over specific assets, preventing the debtor from dealing with those assets without the consent of the secured creditor.  It gives the secured creditor a first claim on the proceeds of sale, and the creditor can usually appoint a receiver to realise the assets in the event of default.

**Floating Charge** – A floating charge is a form of security granted to a creditor over general assets of a company which may change from time to time in the normal course of business (e.g. stock).  The company can continue to use the assets in its business until an event of default occurs and the charge crystallises.  If this happens, the secured creditor can realise the assets to recover his debt, usually by appointing an administrative receiver, and obtain the net proceeds of sale subject to the prior claims of the preferential creditors.

**Fraudulent Trading** – Fraudulent trading involves a company which has carried on business with intent to defraud creditors, or for any fraudulent purpose.  It is a criminal offence and those involved can be made personally liable for the company's liabilities.

**Going Concern** – A going concern is the basis on which Licensed Insolvency Practitioner s prefer to sell a business.  Effectively it means the business continues, jobs are saved, and a higher price is obtained.

**Guarantee** – A guarantee is a legal commitment to repay a debt if the original borrower fails to do so.  Directors may give guarantees to banks in return for the bank giving finance to their companies.

**Individual Voluntary Arrangement (IVA)** – A voluntary arrangement for an individual is a procedure whereby a scheme of arrangement of his affairs or composition in satisfaction of his debts is put forward to creditors.  Such a scheme requires the approval of the court and is under the control of a supervisor.

**Insolvency** – Insolvency is defined as having insufficient assets to meet all debts, or being unable to pay debts as and when they are due.  If a creditor can establish either test, they will be able to present a winding-up petition.  For a bankruptcy petition, inability to pay is the only available ground.

**Insolvency Act 1986** – The Insolvency Act 1986 is the primary legislation governing insolvency law and practice.  Nevertheless, many other statutes and statutory instruments are also relevant.

**Insolvency Services Account** – The Insolvency Services account is an account maintained at the Bank of England by the Department of Trade and Industry, for handling funds in liquidations and bankruptcies.

**Insolvent Liquidation** – A company goes into insolvent liquidation if it goes into liquidation at a time when its assets are insufficient for the payment of its debts and other liabilities and the expenses of liquidation.

**Insolvent Partnerships Order 1994 (IPO)** – The Insolvent Partnerships Order 1994 is an Order setting out the procedures for dealing with insolvent partnerships. The order provides for winding up an insolvent partnership as an unregistered company, with or without concurrent insolvency proceedings against individual partners; for the joint bankruptcy of individual partners, without winding up the partnership as an unregistered company; and for the application of the administration and company voluntary arrangement procedures to insolvent partnerships.

**Interim Order** – An individual who intends to propose a voluntary arrangement to his creditors may apply to the court for an interim order which, if granted, precludes bankruptcy and other legal proceedings while the order is in force.

**Judge in Chambers** – This is a judge sitting informally in his offices (chambers) instead of a Court.

**Judgement** – A judgement is:
1. Recognition of a debt by a court.
2. Decision given by a court at the conclusion of a trial.

**Law of Property Act 1925** – The Law of Property Act 1925 governs transactions in law and property. Contains statutory powers of receivers appointed under a fixed charge.

**Law of Property Act Receiver** – The Law of Property Act 1925 receiver is a person (not necessarily an insolvency practitioner) appointed to take charge of a mortgaged property by a lender whose loan is in default, usually with a view to sale or to collect rental income for the lender. This is common in the case of the failure of a property developer, whose borrowings will largely be secured on specific properties.

**Licensed Insolvency Practitioner (IP)** – A Licensed Insolvency Practitioner (IP) is a person licensed by one of the Chartered Accountancy bodies, the Law Societies, the Insolvency

Practitioners' Association or the Secretary of State for Trade and Industry. They are the only person who may act as an office holder in an insolvency. Persons claiming to be insolvency practitioners, but who do not hold a licence may not be able to help you.

**Lien** – Lien is the right to retain possession of assets or documents until the settlement of a debt.

**Liquidation (Winding Up)** – Liquidation is the process whereby a company has its assets realised and distributed to satisfy, insofar as it is able, its liabilities and to repay its shareholders. The term winding up is also used. Liquidation is usually a terminal process, followed by the dissolution of the company.

**Liquidation Committee** – A liquidations committee is a committee which receives information from the liquidator and sanctions some of his actions. Usually consists entirely of creditors, but may also comprise shareholders (see Creditors' Committee).

**Liquidator** – A liquidator is a Licensed Insolvency Practitioner appointed to wind up a company.

**Mareva Injunction** – A Mareva Injunction is a court order preventing the disposal of assets.

**Member (of a company)** – A person who has agreed to be, and is registered as, a member, such as a shareholder of a limited company.

**Members' Voluntary Liquidation (MVL)** – A members' voluntary liquidation is a solvent liquidation where the shareholders appoint the liquidator to realise assets and settle all the company's debts, plus interest, in full within 12 months.

**Misfeasance** – Misfeasance is a breach of duty in relation to the funds or property of a company by its directors or managers.

**Mortgage** – A mortgage is a transfer of an interest in land or other property by way of security, upon the express or implied condition that the asset shall be reconveyed to the debtor when the sum secured has been paid.

**Nominee** – A nominee is a Licensed Insolvency Practitioner nominated in a proposal for an individual or company voluntary arrangement to act as supervisor of the arrangement.

**Office Holder** – An office holder is a liquidator, provisional liquidator, administrator, administrative receiver, supervisor of a voluntary arrangement, or trustee in bankruptcy.

**Officer (of a Company)** – This is a director, manager or secretary of a company.

**Official Receiver (OR)** – An official receiver (OR) is an officer of the court, civil servant, member of the Department of Trade Insolvency Service and deals with bankruptcies and compulsory liquidations.

**Onerous Property** – The term onerous property in the context of a liquidation or bankruptcy, applies to unprofitable contracts and to property that is unsaleable or not easily saleable or that might give rise to a continuing liability. Such property can be disclaimed by a liquidator or a trustee in bankruptcy.

**Partnership Voluntary Arrangement** – The term used informally to describe the company voluntary arrangement procedure as applied to partnerships under the provisions of The Insolvent Partnerships Order 1994.

**Person** – An individual or corporation.

**Petition** – A petition is a written application to the court for relief or remedy.

**Preference** – A preference is a payment or other transaction made by an insolvent company or individual which places the receiving creditor in a better position than they would have been otherwise. A liquidator, administrator or trustee in bankruptcy may recover sums which are found to be preferences, if the transactions took place within a period of either two years (where the creditor is a connected person) or six months (in other cases) of the insolvency.

**Preferential Debts** – These are defined in Schedule 6 of The Insolvency Act 1986. They have priority when funds are distributed by a liquidator, administrator, administrative receiver or trustee in bankruptcy.

**Proof of Debt** – Proof of debt is a document submitted by a creditor to the Licensed Insolvency Practitioner or Official Receiver giving evidence of the amount of the debt.

**Provisional Liquidator** – Provisional liquidator is the name usually given to a Licensed Insolvency Practitioner appointed, to safeguard a company's assets after presentation of a winding-up petition but before a winding-up order is made.

**Proxy** – A proxy is a document by which a creditor authorises another person to represent him at a meeting of creditors. The proxy may be a general proxy, giving the proxy holder discretion as to how they vote, or a special proxy requiring them to vote as directed by the creditor. A body corporate can only be represented by a proxy.

**Proxy Form** – Form that must be completed if a creditor wishes someone else to represent him or her at a creditors meeting and vote on his or her behalf.

**Proxy Holder** – A proxy holder is a person who attends a meeting on behalf of someone else.

**Public Examination** – When a company is being wound up or in bankruptcy proceedings, the Official Receiver may at any time apply to the court to question the company's director(s) or any other person who has taken part in the promotion, formation or management of the company or the bankrupt.

Realise – Realising an asset means selling it or disposing of it to raise money, for example to sell an insolvent's assets and obtain the proceeds.

**Receiver** – A receiver is often used to describe an administrative receiver, who may be Appointed by a secured creditor holding a floating charge over a company's assets. More accurately, a receiver is the person appointed by a secured creditor holding a fixed charge over specific assets of a company in order to take control of those assets for the benefit of the secured creditor.

**Receivership** – A receivership is the general term applied when a person is appointed as a receiver or administrative receiver.

**Recognised Professional Body (RPB)** – A recognised professional body is an organisation recognised by the Secretary of State for Trade and Industry as being able to authorise its members to act as Licensed Insolvency Practitioners.

**Release** – The process by which the Official Receiver or an insolvency practitioner is discharged from the liabilities of office as trustee/liquidator or administrator.

**Relevant Date** – A relevant date is the date by reference to which preferential claims are reckoned.

**Reservation of Title (or Retention of Title)** – Reservation of title (or retention of title) is a provision under a contract for the supply of goods which purports to reserve ownership of the goods with the supplier until the goods have been paid for. This is a complex and continually evolving area of law.

**Rescission** – A procedure that cancels a winding-up order.

**Scheme of Arrangement** – A scheme of arrangement is a term normally used to describe a compromise or arrangement between a company and its creditors or members or any class of them under section 425 of the Companies Act 1985, which may involve a scheme for the reconstruction of the company. If a majority in number representing three fourths in value of the creditors or members or any class of them agree to the compromise or arrangement it is binding if sanctioned by the court. Section 425 may be invoked where there is an administration order in force in relation to the company, where there is a liquidator or provisional liquidator in office, or where the company is not subject to any insolvency proceedings.

The term is also used in Section 1 of the Insolvency Act 1986 in relation to company voluntary arrangements.

**Secretary of State** - The Secretary of State for the Department for Business, Enterprise and Regulatory Reform.

**Secured Creditor** - A secured creditor is a creditor with specific rights over some or all of a debtor's assets. A secured creditor gets paid first out of the proceeds of sale of the security.

**Security** - A security is a charge or mortgage over assets taken to secure payment of a debt. If the debt is not paid, the lender has a right to sell the charged assets. Security documents can be very complex. The commonest example is a mortgage over a property.

**Shadow Director** - A shadow director is a person who is not formally appointed as a director, but in accordance with whose directions or instructions the directors of a company are accustomed to act. However, a person is not a shadow director merely because the directors act on advice given by him in a professional capacity.

**Special Manager** - A special manager is a person appointed by the court in a compulsory liquidation or bankruptcy to assist the liquidator, Official Receiver or trustee in managing the insolvent's business. They do not need to be a Licensed Insolvency Practitioner .

**Statement of Affairs** – This is a document sworn under oath, completed by a bankrupt, company officer or director(s), stating the assets and giving details of debts and creditors.

**Statutory Demand** – A statutory demand is a formal notice requiring payment of a debt exceeding £750 within 21 days, in default of which bankruptcy or liquidation proceedings may be commenced without further notice. This cannot be used where the debt is disputed.

**Supervision, Court** – All actions must be supervised by the Court.

**Supervisor** – A supervisor is the Licensed Insolvency Practitioner appointed by creditors to supervise the way in which an approved voluntary arrangement is put into effect.

**Transaction at an Undervalue** – A transaction at an undervalue can describe either a gift or a transaction in which the consideration received is significantly less than that given. In certain circumstances such a transaction can be challenged by an administrator, a liquidator or a trustee in bankruptcy.

**Trustee** – Quite apart from its common usage (e.g. under the Trustee Act 1925) this is a term used for a variety of insolvency appointments, including the Licensed Insolvency Practitioner appointed in an English bankruptcy, a Scottish sequestration, a deed of arrangement; a Scottish trust deed and an administration order (of the affairs of a deceased debtor).

**UNCITRAL** – United Nations Commission on International Trade Law.

**Undervalue Transaction** – See Transaction at an Undervalue.

**Unsecured Creditor** – An unsecured creditor, strictly, is any creditor who does not hold security. More commonly used to refer to any ordinary creditor who has no preferential rights, although, in fact preferential creditors will almost always also have an element that is unsecured. In any event, they are the last in the queue, apart from shareholders.

**VAT Bad Debt Relief** – VAT Bad Debt Relief is the relief obtained in respect of the VAT element of an unpaid debt. Previously available only when the debtor became insolvent, relief is now available where debt is six months old at the relevant date.

**Voluntary Arrangements** – See Individual Voluntary Arrangement (IVA) and Company Voluntary Arrangement (CVA).

**Voluntary Liquidation** – See Creditors' Voluntary Liquidation and Members' Voluntary Liquidation.

**Winding up** – See Liquidation.

**Winding-up Order** – A winding-up order is an order made by the court for a company to be placed in compulsory liquidation.

**Winding-up Petition** – A winding-up petitions is a petition presented to the court seeking an order that a company be put into compulsory liquidation.

**Wrongful Trading** – Wrongful trading is a term applied to companies in liquidation where a director allowed the company to continue trading in circumstances where they should have concluded that there was no reasonable prospect that the company would avoid going into insolvent liquidation. The directors involved may be made personally liable to make a contribution to the company's assets.

# Index